Allan Pinkerton

The Detective and the Somnambulist

The Murderer and the Fortune Teller

Allan Pinkerton

The Detective and the Somnambulist
The Murderer and the Fortune Teller

ISBN/EAN: 9783337267346

Printed in Europe, USA, Canada, Australia, Japan

Cover: Foto ©ninafisch / pixelio.de

More available books at **www.hansebooks.com**

THE DETECTIVE

AND THE

SOMNAMBULIST.

THE MURDERER

AND

THE FORTUNE TELLER.

By ALLAN PINKERTON,

AUTHOR OF "THE EXPRESSMAN AND THE DETECTIVE," "CLAUDE MELNOTTE,"
ETC., ETC., ETC.

TORONTO:
BELFORD BROTHERS.
1877.

PREFACE

IN presenting to the public my third volume of Detective Stories, I desire to again call attention to the fact that the stories herein contained, as in the case of their predecessors in the series, are literally true. The incidents in these cases have all actually occurred as related, and there are now living many witnesses to corroborate my statements.

Maroney, the expressman, is living in Georgia, having been released during the war. Mrs. Maroney is also alive. Any one desiring to convince himself of the absolute truthfulness of this narrative can do so by examining the court records in Montgomery, Ala., where Maroney was convicted.

The facts stated in the second volume are well known to many residents of Chicago. Young Bright was in the best society during his stay at the Clifton House, and many of his friends will remember him. His father is now largely interested in business in New York, Chicago, and St. Louis. The events connected with the abduction of "The Two Sisters," will be readily recalled by W. L. Church, Esq., of Chicago, and others. The story of "Alexander Gay," the Frenchman, will be found in the criminal records of St. Louis, where he was sentenced for forgery.

So with the stories in this volume. The characters in "The Detective and the Somnambulist," will be easily recognized by many readers in the South. As the family of Drysdale are still living and holding a highly respectable place in society, the locality is not correctly given, and fictitious names are used throughout.

By reason of the peculiar nature of the circumstances, the facts narrated in "The Murderer and the Fortune-Teller," are known only to a small circle, but they can readily be substantiated. Captain Sumner was never informed of the means employed to influence his sister, and his first knowledge of them will be obtained in reading this book; but he will remember his own visit to "Lucille," and will undoubtedly see that the affair was managed exactly as I have stated.

In reading these stories, the reader will probably come to the conclusion that the detection of criminals is a very simple matter, and that any one with a moderate amount of intelligence could have done just as well. To a certain extent this is true, but not wholly. The plan once adopted, it is not difficult to put it in execution; but experience, judgment and tact are required to form a plan which will bring out the real facts connected with the crime. This done, the capture of the criminal is only a question of time.

Legitimate, honest detective business is yet in its infancy, but the trade, as at present generally conducted, approaches the dignity of an art—a black art, unfortunately, the object being accurately to distinguish the percentage of plunder which will satisfy the criminals and the real owners, the remainder being divided among the so-called detectives.

In point of fact, these fellows are worse than the acknowledged criminals, since they rob under the guise of honest men, and run little or no risk, while the actual thieves take their lives in their hands. It may safely be said that the average detective would rather be in league with the criminals of this city than opposed to them, and the great majority *are* so leagued; and until such a state of affairs is broken up, the criminals who have money will surely escape punishment.

ALLAN PINKERTON.

September, 1875.

THE DETECTIVE

AND THE

SOMNAMBULIST.

CHAPTER I.

ABOUT nineteen years ago, I was enjoying a short relaxation from the usual press of business in Chicago. I had only one or two really important cases on hand, and I was therefore preparing to take a much needed rest. At this time, my business was not nearly so extensive as it has since become, nor was my Agency so well known as it now is; hence, I was somewhat surprised and gratified to receive a letter from Atkinson, Mississippi, asking me to go to that town at once, to investigate a great crime recently perpetrated there. I had intended to visit my former home in Dundee, for a week or ten days, but, on receiving this letter, I postponed my vacation indefinitely.

The letter was written by Mr. Thomas McGregor, cashier of the City Bank, of Atkinson, and my services were called for by all the officers of the bank. The circumstances of the case were, in brief, that the paying-teller had been brutally murdered in the bank about three or four months before, and over one hundred and thirty thousand dollars had been stolen. Mr. McGregor said that no expense should be spared to detect the criminals, even though the money was not recovered; that would be an important consideration, of course, but the first object sought was the capture of the murderers of poor George Gordon, the late paying-teller.

Having already arranged my business for a brief absence, I was all ready for the journey, and by the next train, I was speeding southward, toward Atkinson.

I arrived there early in the morning, of one of the most delightful days of early spring. I had exchanged the brown fields and bare trees of the raw and frosty North, for the balmy airs, blooming flowers, and waving foliage of the sunny South. The contrast was most agreeable to me in my then tired and overworked condition, and I felt that a few days in that climate would restore my strength more effectually than a stay of several weeks in the changeable and inclement weather of northern Illinois. For sanitary, as well as business reasons, therefore, I had no occasion to regret my Southern trip.

My assumed character was that of a cotton speculator, and I was thus able to make many inquiries relative to the town and its inhabitants, without exciting suspicion. Of course, I should have considerable business at the bank, and thus, I could have frequent conferences with the bank officials, without betraying my real object in visiting them. I sent a note to Mr. McGregor, on my arrival, simply announcing myself under a fictitious name, and I soon received a reply requesting me to come to the bank at eight o'clock that evening. I then spent the day in walking about the town and gathering a general idea of the surroundings of the place.

Atkinson was then a town of medium size, pleasantly situated near the northern boundary of the State. The surrounding country was well watered and wooded, consisting of alternate arable land and rolling hills. The inhabitants of the town were divided into two general classes : the shop-keepers, mechanics, and laborers, formed the bulk of the population; while the capitalists, planters and professional men were the most influential. Most of these latter owned country residences, or plantations outside of the town, though they kept up their town establishments also. A small water-course, called Rocky Creek, skirted one side of the place, and many of the most handsome houses, were situated on, or near this beautiful rivulet. The whole appearance of Atkinson, and the surrounding country, indicated a thrifty, well-to-do population.

Having roamed about to my satisfaction, I spent the latter part of the afternoon at the hotel, where I met a number of the professional men of the county. I found that the hotel was occupied by many of the best families during the winter and spring, and I soon formed the acquaintance of several of the gentlemen. They greeted me with characteristic Southern hospitality, and I was pleased to see that my *role* as a Scotch speculator was quite an easy one to play; at least, no one ever appeared to suspect my real object in visiting Atkinson.

At the appointed hour I went to the bank, and was met

outside by Mr. McGregor, to whom I had been introduced during the day. He took me in through the private entrance, and we were joined in a few minutes by Alexander Bannatine, president, and Peter A. Gordon, vice-president, of the bank. Mr. Bannatine was about fifty years of age, but he looked much older, owing to his continuous and exhausting labors as a lawyer, during the early part of his life. Having made a large fortune by successful practice and judicious investments, he had retired from the active pursuit of his profession, and had joined several old friends in the banking business. Mr. Gordon was, also, about fifty years old. He had become wealthy by inheritance, and had increased his fortune by twenty years of careful attention to business. He was unmarried, and George Gordon, the murdered bank-teller, had stood in the relation of a son to his uncle; hence, there was an additional reason for the capture and conviction of the murderers. The recovery of the large sum of money stolen, would, alone, have been an important consideration, but Mr. Gordon was willing to spend a very extravagant amount in the detection of the criminals, even though the money might never be discovered.

We seated ourselves at a table in the cashier's room, and I prepared to take notes of all the facts then known by the gentlemen present.

"Now, Mr. Bannatine," I said, "please tell me everything connected with the case, which may be of service to me."

"Well, Mr. Pinkerton, I have not been connected with the bank so long, or so closely as Mr. McGregor," said

Mr. Bannatine, "and perhaps he had better give a short sketch of young Gordon's connection with the bank first."

"George Gordon was taken into our employ about five years ago," said Mr. McGregor. "He had previously acted as our agent in one of the interior towns, and when he became of age he was offered the place of paying-teller. Since then his obliging disposition, courteous manners, and faithful performance of duty, have endeared him to all his associates, and have given him the confidence of all persons with whom he came in contact. His character was spotless, and his devotion to duty was superior to all allurements; he would never sacrifice one moment to pleasure which should have been given to business."

"Had he any associates among the fast men and women of the place?" I asked.

"No, sir, not one," was the prompt reply; "we have not been able to learn that he had any acquaintances even, among that class."

"Well, please proceed to state all the circumstances connected with the murder," I suggested.

"I was not at home at the time," said Mr. McGregor, "but I can give you many facts, and Mr. Gordon can add thereto. George was in the habit of remaining in the bank after office hours for the purpose of writing up his books, as he acted as book-keeper also. During the very busy seasons, he would sometimes be kept at work until long after dark, though this was unusual. Occasionally customers would come to the bank after the regular hours, and George would accommodate them, or I would do so, when I was present. We were both very careful about admitting outsiders after the bank had closed, and we never allowed any one to enter except well-known business men and old customers of the bank. We had large sums on hand at times, and George frequently said that we could not exercise too much care in managing our business. I mention this to show that he was not careless in his habits, but that, on the contrary, he always took the greatest precautions against fraud or violence."

"Were there any customers who were in the habit of coming in late?" I asked.

"Yes, there were several," replied Mr. McGregor; "for instance, Mr. Flanders, the jeweler, used to bring over his more valuable jewelry every afternoon to put into our vault; he would put it into a small box and leave it here about five o'clock. Then, our county clerk, Mr. Drysdale, used to stop frequently to make deposits in cases where other parties had paid money to him after banking hours. He was very intimate with George, and he used to stop to see him sometimes and walk out with him after his work was finished. Walter Patterson, also, was one of George's particular friends, and he has often stayed with George until nine or ten o'clock in the evening. Besides these there were several of our leading planters who would come in as late as eight o'clock to deposit funds, or to obtain cash for use early the next day."

"Did young Gordon have the keys to the vault?" I asked.

"Oh! yes," replied Mr. McGregor; "I was often called away on business for several days, and he used to act as cashier in my absence. He was in the habit of carrying the keys with him at all times; but his uncle advised him not to do so, as they might be taken from him by a gang of desperate characters, and the bank robbed. He had, therefore, given up the practice of taking the keys home with him after night-fall. Just about the time of the murder, we had one of the busiest seasons ever known; the cotton crop had been enormous, and sales had been very rapid, so that our deposits were unusually large. One morning I found that I must go to Greenville for several days, on business of great importance. Before going, I gave George full instructions upon all matters which might need attention during my absence; yet I felt, while on my way to the depot, that there was something which I had forgotten. I could not define what it was, but I hurried back to ask whether he could think of any thing further upon which he might wish my advice. I found him chatting with his friend, Mr. Drysdale. Calling him to one side, I said:

"'George, is there anything more upon which I can advise you?'

"'No, I guess not,' he replied; 'you will be back so soon that if there should anything new turn up, it can wait until you return.'

"'Well, be very careful,' I continued, 'and don't allow any one to come in here after dark. It may be an unnecessary precaution, but I should feel easier if I knew no one was admitted to the bank during my absence.'

"'Very well,' he replied, 'I shall allow only one or two of my personal friends to come in. There will be no harm in admitting them, for they will be an additional protection in case of any attempt on the bank.'

"I could offer no objection, and so we parted. I was gone about a week, when, having settled my business in

Greenville, I returned here. The first news I received was, that George Gordon had been found murdered in the bank that morning, the crime having been committed the night before. I will now let Mr. Peter Gordon, George's uncle, tell the circumstances, so far as he knows them."

Mr. McGregor was a careful, methodical man, about sixty years of age. He always spoke directly to the point, and in his story, he had evidently made no attempt to draw conclusions, or to bias my judgment in any way. Nevertheless, he showed that he was really affected by young Gordon's murder, and I saw that I should get more really valuable assistance from him, than from both of the other two. Mr. Gordon was greatly excited, and he could hardly speak at times, as he thought of his murdered nephew. His story was told slowly and painfully, as if the details were almost too much for him. Still, he felt that nothing ought to be neglected which would assist me, and so he nerved himself to tell every little incident of the dreadful crime.

"I remember the day of the murder very distinctly, Mr. Pinkerton," he said. "Mr. Bannatine was obliged to visit his plantation that morning, and Mr. McGregor being away, as he has already told you, I spent most of the day at the bank with George. He was perfectly competent to manage all the business himself, Mr. Pinkerton, for he was a very smart and trustworthy young man, the very image of my dear brother, who was drowned twenty years ago, leaving me to bring up George like my own son; but, as I was saying, I kept George company in the bank that day, more as a measure of safety, than because he needed me. Well, we received a large amount of money that day in bank notes and specie, and I helped George put the money into the vault. When the bank closed, George said that he should work until five o'clock and then go home to dinner. I was anxious to go to my store, as business had been very heavy that day, and I had had no opportunity to attend to my own affairs; I therefore left the bank at four o'clock. George and I boarded at the hotel, and at dinner time, he came late, so that I finished before he did. About seven o'clock, George came down to the store, where I had gone after dinner. He sat a little while and smoked a cigar with me, and then said that he must return to the bank, as he had a great deal of work to finish up on the books; he told me, also, not to sit up for him, as it might be quite late before he came home."

"Were there any other persons present when he said this, Mr. Gordon?" I asked.

"Yes; there was a shoemaker, named Stolz, whom George had just paid for a pair of boots. Mr. Flanders, the jeweler, was there also, and he had his box of jewelry for George to lock up in the safe. There had been so many customers in his store that afternoon that he had not been able to take the box over before. There were several other persons present, I recollect now that you ask me about it, but I had not thought of the matter before, and I cannot recall their names."

"Well, I guess we can find out," I replied; "please go on. By the way, one question: had George drank anything at all during the day?"

"No, sir, nothing whatever. George used to smoke a great deal, but he *never* drank at a bar in his life; all his young friends will tell you the same. He sometimes drank wine at meals at his own or a friend's table, but he never drank at any other place. He left my store about half-past seven o'clock, and Flanders went with him to leave his jewelry. Flanders' store is near mine, and he soon came back and chatted with me a short time. He has since told me that he did not enter the bank, but that he simply handed the case of jewelry to George on the steps of the private entrance, and George said to him: 'I won't ask you to come in, Flanders, for I have too much work to attend to, and I can't entertain you.' These are the last words that George is known to have spoken."

Here Mr. Gordon's agitation was so great that he could not speak for several minutes, but at length, he continued:

"I went to bed about ten o'clock that evening, and came down late to breakfast next morning. I did not see George anywhere around the hotel, but I thought nothing of that, as I supposed that he had gone to the bank. After breakfast, I got shaved, smoked a cigar, and then went to my store. In a few minutes, a man named Rollo, who has an account at the bank, came in and said:

"'Mr. Gordon, what is the matter at the bank this morning? It is now after ten o'clock, and everything is still shut up.'

"'What!' I exclaimed, 'the bank not opened yet! My nephew must be sick, though he was quite well yesterday evening. I will go to the bank with you at once, Mr. Rollo.'

"One of my clerks accompanied us, and on arriving at the bank, we found a cabinet-maker named Breed, trying to get in. I went and pounded on the front door several

"At this instant I flung open one of the shutters, and simultaneously I heard a cry of horror from my clerk." — Page 19.

times, but no one came. I then went to the private entrance and gave the signal by rapping, to let those inside know that one of the bank officers was at the door. We had a private signal known only to the officers, so that I was sure there must be something wrong when I found it unanswered. I had a dreadful feeling in my heart that something horrible had happened, and I was about to hurry away to the hotel, to see if George was there, when I casually let my hand fall upon the knob and turned it; to my surprise, the door yielded.

"By this time, quite a crowd had gathered outside, attracted by the unusual spectacle of the closed bank, and the knocking at the doors. I therefore left Mr. Rollo and Mr. Breed to keep the crowd from entering the side entrance, while my clerk and I threw open the heavy shutters of this room where we are now sitting. We then entered the main bank through yonder door, and while I went to open the outside blinds, which excluded every particle of light, my clerk walked down behind the bank counter. He suddenly stumbled over something and fell, and as he got up, he said that the floor was wet. At this instant, I flung open one of the shutters, and simultaneously I heard a cry of horror from my clerk. Running to the counter, I looked over and saw a terrible sight. My poor boy—"

Again Mr Gordon's feelings overcame him, and it was some time before he could go on. Finally he was able to resume his story, though he was frequently obliged to pause to wipe away his tears.

"My nephew's body was lying midway between his desk and the vault door; he had evidently been standing at his desk when he was struck, as was shown by the direction in which the blood had spirted. He had been murdered by three blows on the back of the head, the instrument used being a heavy canceling hammer, which we found close by, clotted with blood and hair. The first blow had been dealt just back of the left ear while George was standing at his desk; he had then staggered backward two or three steps before falling, and the second and third blows had been struck as he lay on the floor. Although it was evident that the first blow alone was sufficient to cause death, the murderer had been anxious to complete his work beyond any possibility of failure.

"The scene was most ghastly; George's body lay in a pool of blood, while the desks, chairs, table and wall, were spattered with large drops which had spirted out as the blows were struck. I shall never forget that terrible morning, and sometimes I awake with a horrible choking sensation, and think that I have just renewed the sickening experience of that day.

"Well, I immediately suspected that the murder had been committed to enable the murderer to rob the bank. I knew that George had no enemies who would seek his life, and there could be no other object in killing him inside the bank. The outer door of the vault stood slightly ajar, and as soon as I had satisfied myself that my nephew was dead—as indeed was evident, the body being quite cold—I sent my clerk to call Mr. Rollo and Mr. Breed into the bank, while he remained at the door. I told him to send any person whom he might see outside for the sheriff and the coroner. As I was saying, the vault door stood slightly open, and when the other gentlemen joined me I called their attention to the position of everything before I entered the vault. I found the keys in the lock of the inner door, and on opening the latter we saw that everything inside was in great confusion. Without making any examination, I closed and locked both doors, and sealed the key-holes with tape and sealing-wax. I determined to leave everything just as it was until the inquest should be held. The sheriff and coroner soon arrived, and a jury was impaneled immediately, as, by that time, the news had spread all over town, and the bank was surrounded by nearly all the best men in the place. In summoning the jury, the coroner put down for foreman the name of Mr. Drysdale, George's most intimate friend, but it was found that he was not in the crowd outside, and when they sent for him he begged so hard to be excused that he was let off.

"The inquest was held in this room, but nothing was moved from the bank except the body and the canceling hammer. The jury elicited nothing more than what I have told you, and they therefore adjourned to await the examination of our vault when Mr. McGregor and Mr. Bannatine returned, in the hope that some clue might be found therein. I forgot to mention that we found in George's hand a bill of the Planters' Bank of Georgia, of the denomination of one hundred dollars. It was clutched tightly, and he had fallen on that side, so that the murderer had not noticed it. Here it is, partly stained with blood," and Mr. Gordon handed me a bank note. He then continued:

"A messenger had been dispatched to inform Mr. Bannatine of the disaster, and he arrived in town almost simultaneously with Mr. McGregor, who was already on his way home when the murder occurred. As Mr. Bannatine is well acquainted with all the subsequent events, I prefer that he should give the account of our action since that time."

It was clearly very painful to Mr. Gordon to talk upon the subject of his nephew's murder, and Mr. Bannatine willingly took up the thread of the story. He had practiced at the bar so long that his style resembled that of a witness under examination, and he was always careful to give his authority whenever he stated facts outside of his own observation. His testimony was of the greatest importance to me, and I took very full notes as he went along.

CHAPTER II.

I RECEIVED the intelligence of George Gordon's murder about noon, by a messenger from Mr. Gordon. I immediately rode into town and went to the bank, where I arrived about two o'clock. The inquest was not completed, but at the sheriff's suggestion the jury adjourned until the next morning. The cause of death, according to the testimony of Dr. Hartman and Dr. Larimore, was concussion of the brain, produced by three separate blows on the back of the head; the blows might have been dealt with the canceling hammer, which, Mr. Gordon said, had been found close by the body. The latter was removed to the hotel preparatory to the funeral.

"Mr. Gordon, Mr. McGregor, and myself then proceeded to open the bank, taking the sheriff to assist us in searching for clues to aid in the detection of the criminals. We first opened all the shutters to give as much light as possible. We then examined the interior of the bank; outside of the counter nothing whatever was found, but inside we discovered several important traces of the murderer. The fireplace showed that something had recently been burned in it. The grate had been perfectly clean all summer, and Mr. Gordon tells me such was the case when he left the bank at four o'clock. The character of the ashes—as I am assured by expert chemists—denoted that clothing had been burned, and while examining them I found several buttons; here they are," he added, producing four or five iron buttons, and the charred remains of two or three horn buttons.

"While feeling around in the light ashes beneath the grate," continued Mr. Bannatine, "I found a piece of paper twisted up and charred at one end; its appearance indicated that it had been used to light the fire in the grate. On unrolling it carefully, it proved to be a fragment of a note for $927.78; the signature, part of the date, and the amount of the note were left uncharred, but most of the upper portion was wholly burned. The signature was that of Alexander P. Drysdale, our esteemed county clerk."

Mr. Bannatine here showed me this fragment pressed out between two oblong pieces of heavy plate glass. I glanced at it a few minutes, and then placed it beside the buttons for future examination.

"Among the few scraps of paper found," resumed Mr. Bannatine, "was another one, which we found under George's body, saturated with blood. The murderer had evidently destroyed every piece of paper that he could find; but this one had probably been lying on the floor, and when George fell, it was hidden by his body. This, and the note, were the only papers found on the desks or about the floor of the bank which had any writing upon them; even the waste paper baskets and their contents had been burned. Here is the paper, Mr. Pinkerton; we have preserved it carefully, because we thought that it might suggest something to a detective, though it had no special significance to us."

He handed me the paper, as he spoke. It was a fragment of letter paper, about three by six inches in size. It was stained a brownish red by poor young Gordon's life-blood; but beneath the stain, were plainly visible the pen marks of the murdered man. It had a number of figures on one side, arranged like examples in addition, though they were scattered carelessly, as if he had been checking off balances, and had used this fragment to verify his additions. The reverse side was blank. I laid this paper beside the note, and Mr. Bannatine continued his story:

"We then opened the safe, and counted the money; this was easily done, for we found that all the loose money was gone, leaving only a small quantity of coin and a number of packages of bills. These latter were put up in lots of five thousand dollars each, and were wrapped in a bright red tissue paper. George had put up over one hundred thousand dollars in this way, about a week before, and the murderer had not touched these packages at all: we were thus spared a loss, which would have somewhat crippled us. As it was, the loss in bills amounted to about one hundred and five thousand dollars, while exactly twenty-eight thousand dollars in gold eagles and double eagles, were also missing. A few days after the murder, one of Col. Garnett's slaves found two twenty-dollar gold pieces at an old fording place on Rocky Creek, just outside the city, and we came to the conclusion that the robber had dropped them there; but of course, we could not identify gold pieces, and so we could not be sure. The coroner closed the inquest the following day, and the jury found a verdict of death at the hands of a person or persons unknown. The funeral was attended by people from miles around, and there was a general determination shown to spare no pains to bring the murderers to justice; large rewards were offered by the Governor, by the bank, and by the county officials, and some of the best detectives in the country were employed, but all to no purpose. When the gold pieces were found, a number of George's intimate friends organized a party to search the adjoining woods for traces of the criminals, as it was thought they might have camped out in that vicinity, before or after the deed. All of George's intimate friends joined in the search, except Mr. Drysdale, who was so much overcome at the terrible occurrence, that he was quite prostrated. Nothing was found by this party, however; neither have the various detectives, professional and amateur, who have investigated the case, made the slightest progress toward a solution of the mystery. We have determined to make one more effort, Mr. Pinkerton, and therefore we have sent for you to aid us. It may be that you will see some trace which others have overlooked; you can take whatever steps you choose, and you need spare no expense. If you are successful, we will pay you liberally, besides the rewards offered."

"One of the rules of my Agency," I replied, "forbids the acceptance of rewards; hence, I wish it understood in advance, that my only charges will be according to my regular schedule of prices, and that I expect nothing more. This is my invariable custom, whether the case be one of murder, arson, burglary, or simple theft; the number of detectives, and the time they are employed, will determine the amount I shall charge."

We then arranged the financial portion of our agreement to our mutual satisfaction, and I began my investigations.

"What detectives have you hitherto employed, Mr. Bannatine?" I asked.

"I first laid the matter before two New York detectives, who had been highly recommended to me," he replied; "but they could offer no satisfactory theory to work upon, and after staying here three or four weeks, they said that the murder must have been committed by some member of a gang of gamblers; they thought the murderer would probably go to New Orleans to exchange his money, and that it would be easy to learn by going to that city, whether any gambler had had an unusual amount of money about that time. We were not very well satisfied with this theory, and so the detectives returned to New York. We next engaged two detectives from New Orleans, but they were equally unsuccessful. We then allowed the matter to rest until about a month ago, when we heard such a favorable account of the manner in which you had conducted a case of great difficulty, that we began to discuss the propriety of engaging you in investigating this affair. The more we heard of you, the better we were satisfied, and finally, we authorized Mr. McGregor to write to you on the subject."

"Well, Mr. Bannatine, I shall do my best," I replied, "but you must not expect me to work miracles. Now, I am going to ask you a number of questions, and I wish you to answer them without regard to their apparent drift. Who were George Gordon's intimate friends?"

"Mr. Flanders, Mr. Drysdale, Mr. Patterson, and Mr.

Henry Caruthers; I think they were the only ones he was really very intimate with; isn't it so, Mr. Gordon?"

"Yes; George had very few cronies," replied Mr. Gordon.

"Who is Mr. Caruthers?" I asked.

"He is the son of a wealthy planter living a few miles from town," replied Mr. Bannatine.

"Where was he the afternoon previous to the murder?"

"He came into the bank for a few minutes," said Mr. Gordon, "and asked George to spend Sunday with him on the plantation; then he rode home."

"Were there any strange men in or about the bank that day?"

"None, so far as we could learn; nearly every person that I can recollect having seen that day was a customer, or a townsman whom I knew."

"When George gave up carrying the safe keys home with him, where did he leave them?"

"There is a secret drawer in that desk, which opens by pressing this knob, thus," said Mr. McGregor, suiting the action to the word; "we used to keep the keys there."

"Did any one beside you four gentlemen know this hiding place?"

"I am sure that no one else knew it," said Mr. McGregor.

"Was it necessary for George to open the safe that night, or could he have done his work without going into the vault at all?"

"He had work to do on the journal and ledger, and he would have to use the keys to get them out of the vault.

He did not need to open the inner safe where the money was, however."

"Does the outer vault key open both doors?"

"No; but they were kept on the same chain for convenience."

"Were the ledger and journal on George's desk when you entered the bank, Mr. Gordon?"

"No, sir; they were put away in their usual places in the vault."

"Did they show any marks of blood?"

"None at all; they were perfectly clean."

"Could you tell from their appearance whether George had done any work upon them that night?"

"Yes; I am sure he had done a great deal; in fact he had finished up all entries to date."

"Were there any papers missing besides the money?"

"Yes; one or two bundles of old checks, drafts, etc., were used to assist in burning the murderer's clothes. They were fastened in packages with fine wire, and we found the wire in the grate."

"Then this note, signed 'Alexander P. Drysdale,' might have been pulled out of one of these packages?"

"I suppose so; I don't know where else it came from; do you, Mr. McGregor?" said Mr. Gordon, rather bewildered.

"No; I never thought about where it came from," said Mr. McGregor. "I suppose the man built a fire of old papers and the fragments of the waste paper baskets, and then used that note to set them on fire from the lamp."

"There were no papers of any value used, then?" I continued.

"Oh, no; the papers were old bundles, merely kept as archives of the bank."

I then picked up the note and glanced at it; as I did so, something caught my eye which sent the blood throbbing through my veins at a feverish speed. Enough of the date remained to show that it was drawn some time during the year of the murder, hence it could hardly be one of the archives. Besides, a note, if paid, would be returned to the maker, canceled; if unpaid, it would be kept among the bills receivable, in the inner safe; in neither case could it have been stowed away among the old checks and drafts. This reasoning passed through my mind quickly, and I realized that that little piece of paper might play an important part in the tragedy after all. I did not form any definite theory on the instant, but still I had a sort of presentiment that I had touched a spring which might open the windows of this dark mystery and let in the light of day. I did not show what I thought to my companions, but continued to ask questions.

"Was Mr. Patterson in the bank the day of the murder, Mr. Gordon?"

"Oh, no; he was not in this part of the country at that time; he had been in Mobile for some weeks."

"I understood you to say that Mr. Flanders went no further than the private door with George; did he notice any one standing about when he came away?"

"No; he stopped only an instant, while George unlocked the door, and then gave the jewel box to him to put away. George wished him good night, with the remark that he could not ask him in, as he would be too busy to entertain him. Mr. Flanders then came straight back to my store; but he said at the inquest that he heard George lock the door behind him, and that he saw no one around the building."

"Do you know anything about his circumstances at that time? Was he in need of money?"

"No, indeed; he had a large balance to his credit. Why, surely, you do not see any reason to suspect Mr. Flanders?" said Mr. McGregor.

"I don't say that I suspect anybody," I replied, "but I wish to gather all the information possible. Now, please tell me how large a balance Mr. Flanders had on deposit."

Mr. McGregor immediately examined the ledger for the previous year, and reported that the balance due Mr. Flanders at the time of the murder, was over twelve thousand dollars.

"You see, Mr. Pinkerton," he went on to say, "we balanced our books up to that date, and thus we know just how each person's account stood that day."

"Well, did you find that any of those gentlemen, who were in the habit of entering the bank after business hours, were in debt to the bank, or that they were cramped for money at that time?" I asked, carelessly.

"None of them were in debt to the bank, I know," replied Mr. McGregor; "whether there were any of them in need of money particularly, I cannot say."

"Had any of them tried to borrow from the bank recently?"

"No; in fact, none of them had drawn out the balances due them."

"Please give me a list of their balances on that day," I said; "just give me a memorandum of the amounts standing to each one's credit."

"Whose accounts shall we give you?" asked Mr. McGregor, evidently wondering what object I had in view.

"Well, let me have those of Mr. Flanders, Mr. Patterson, Mr. Drysdale, and Mr. Caruthers; also, let me know whether any of those gentlemen had made any loan from the bank during that year, and if so, the amount, date, etc., and whether a note was given, or security of any kind."

Mr. McGregor, and the other two gentlemen, were completely mystified at my request, but they complied with my wishes, and I noted down the amounts given me in my note-book.

The balances were as follows: Patterson, $2,472.27; Drysdale, $324.22; Caruthers, $817.48; and Flanders, $12,263.03. None of them had made loans from the bank, except Caruthers, who had once overdrawn his account nearly three hundred dollars, but he gave no note, as he was good for any amount. None of the others had given a note to the bank, or to any one else, so far as was known, for several years.

"Now, gentlemen," I said, "please take me into the bank and show me exactly how the place appeared when Mr. Gordon first discovered that George had been murdered."

Mr. Gordon rose with great effort and opened the door connecting the private office with the main bank. It was evidently very painful to him, but he did not shrink. Turning to me, he said:

"Mr. Pinkerton, let Mr. McGregor go first, and light the lamp; I will then proceed just as I did that morning, and will point out the exact position of everything in the bank."

Mr. McGregor accordingly lighted a large lamp, which threw a soft radiance over the whole interior, and the two moved the furniture into the position in which it had been found on that fatal morning. Mr. Gordon then showed me the exact position of the body, the spot where the paper lay, the canceling hammer, and the blood-marks. After I had been shown everything, I stood and thought over the matter in connection with the surroundings, and endeavored to re-enact the scene of the murder in my own mind. Bit by bit, I brought out some of the surroundings to my own satisfaction, and when I went back to the private office, I had a well-defined theory in my mind. Not that I had so narrowed down my suspicions, as to fix them upon any particular individual — I had not yet gone so far — but my theory was fully established, and I felt sure that by working it up carefully, I should soon discover some traces of the guilty party. The officers of the bank followed me in silence, and on resuming our seats, I said:

"Gentlemen, I wish to take a day to weigh the testimony in this case, before I can give you any opinion about it. I would like to take this note, the memorandum, and the buttons to my room, and to-morrow evening I will tell you what conclusions I have reached. Is that satisfactory?"

"Certainly; we do not wish to proceed in haste, Mr. Pinkerton," said Mr. Bannatine; "we will meet you then at the same hour to-morrow."

"I do not wish to seem impatient," said Mr. Gordon, "but can you not tell me now whether you have obtained any clue from what we have told you, which will enable you to learn more?"

Mr. Gordon's anxiety was so keen that I wished to relieve his mind somewhat; but, on the other hand, I did not wish to raise his hopes unnecessarily, lest some unforeseen thing might occur to overthrow my theory entirely. I replied, therefore:

"Mr. Gordon, I may think I have a clue now, which, on mature reflection, may prove worthless; hence, I should prefer to take a day, before giving my opinion."

"You are right, Mr. Pinkerton," he said; "I should feel worse to have my hopes raised, only to be dashed down again, than if I had never expected anything. Take your own time, and then let us know the result."

"There are two questions more, which I would like answered," I said. "Was it possible for any person to have entered the bank by force? That is, were there any indications whatever, to show that the murderer might have possibly gained entrance during George's absence at dinner?"

"No; none at all. The sheriff made a very careful examination of all the windows, and both doors," replied Mr. McGregor. "He thought that a gang of gamblers, who stopped here a few weeks, might have used nippers on the key of the side door after George had locked it, and that they had then stolen upon George, at his desk, and killed him; but, there were no evidences that such was the case."

"Well, did any one, except you three gentlemen, know the private signal by which those inside the bank could tell that the person at the door, was one of the bank officers?"

"I am not sure about that," said Mr. Gordon; "possibly some of our well-known friends might have been with us when we gained admittance to the bank, but I cannot say that I think they ever learned the signal."

"You think, however, that Patterson, Drysdale, Flanders, or Caruthers, *might* have known it?"

"Yes; in fact, on thinking it over, I feel quite sure that Mr. Patterson and Mr. Drysdale did know it."

"Well, I don't think I have any more questions to ask," I said. "I shall be here promptly at eight o'clock to-morrow evening, and if you should wish to communicate with me before that time, send me a message, and I will call at the bank. This will not attract attention, as my business is supposed to be cotton buying, and a visit at the bank will not be considered unusual."

I then took charge of the papers, etc., and went to my room at the hotel. I merely glanced at the buttons, and bank note, hastily, as I knew they could serve only as corroboratory evidence in the event of obtaining a weak chain of proof. I then turned to the note, which I studied long and carefully. I was convinced that it was of recent date, at the time of the murder, although only the last figure of the date was visible. I finally looked over the blood-stained piece of paper, which George had nearly covered with figures. I saw at a glance, that there was no reading matter on it, but I began to go over his figures half mechanically, mentally following his addition, to verify it.

Suddenly my eyes caught two numbers near the bottom of the paper. They were placed together, and their difference was written below; they were much fainter than the rest, having been made in pencil, instead of in ink. It was probably due to this fact, that they had never been noticed before, as the deep stain made it difficult to distinguish them clearly, without close observation. However that may be, they acted upon me like an electric shock, and I was obliged to walk about the room a few minutes, to compose my nerves. It was strange that those faint lines should have told so much, but it seemed almost, as if the murdered man had whispered his murderer's name to me. The numbers which were there set down were $927.78, and $324.22. *One of them was the amount of the half burned note of Drysdale; the other, was the amount of his balance in the bank.*

I sat up until a very late hour, thinking over the possible solution of the mystery, and when I finally went to bed, I had satisfied myself as to the identity of the murderer. The next day, I rose late, and spent the afternoon in arranging the points of evidence in consecutive order, so as to be able to present them to the bank officials in the most convincing manner. I then walked around town for exercise. During my walk, I visited Mr. Flanders' jewelry store and the county clerk's office.

Mr. Flanders was an elderly gentlemen of very mild and courteous manners, and his whole appearance would lead any one to regard it as impossible, that he should have committed murder.

Mr. Drysdale, the county clerk, was a fine looking man, of about forty years of age. He was of the nervous, sanguine type; was quiet and courteous, but haughty and reserved to strangers; he was looking thin and weary, as if he worked too hard, and streaks of gray were just visible in his hair and mustache.

I talked with him for about half an hour, representing that I was a stranger, desirous of gaining information about the plantations of the county. He answered my questions politely, but as briefly as possible, and I saw that my presence, apparently, bored him, and interfered with his duties. As I was about to go, I asked him to write the name and address of some reliable cotton factor in my note-book, and he complied very willingly. I then returned to the hotel, and patiently waited until eight o'clock.

CHAPTER III.

ON going to the bank I found the three gentlemen awaiting me most anxiously. After the usual greeting we seated ourselves at the table. I arranged my notes for convenient reference, and began to state my conclusions:

"Gentlemen, I have approached this case with a great deal of care, and have given it much thought. Aside from the importance of the interests involved, there are other reasons which render me cautious in forming and stating an opinion; other detectives of ability and experience have been baffled; several months have elapsed since the crimes were committed; and, lastly, the theory upon which I have reasoned has led me in such a direction that nothing but the strongest conviction in my own mind would warrant me in making the statement which I am now about to give you. Let me first, then, review the case, and show the chain of evidence as it appears to me:

"George Gordon appears to have been a young man of more than average ability as a bank officer; he was cautious in his habits, and at this particular time he had recently been specially cautioned by Mr. McGregor; consequently it is likely that he would have been unusually careful to admit only those with whom he was very well acquainted. Again, the position of the furniture and the appearance of the blood-marks, show that George was standing at his desk, and that he was struck from behind. Now, he had finished his work on the books and put them away. What, then, was he doing? There is but one thing which throws any light upon this subject —the bank bill which you found in his hand. From its presence I infer that he was engaged in handling money; indeed, I may say that he must have been either receiving it or paying it out. That he was receiving it is not likely, for the murderer was probably short of funds; hence I conclude that he was paying it out. It is also clear that the amount must have been large, as shown by the denomination of the bill—one hundred dollars.

"These facts and inferences lead me to believe that the murderer was a personal friend of George, and a customer of the bank; and I may say that I had reached this conclusion yesterday evening, while listening to the testimony of you three gentlemen, before I had discovered any corroborative evidence. I will now give some of the additional points which I have brought out since then; but I wish that you would first tell me whether this signature is genuine," I said, pointing to Alexander P. Drysdale's name on the note.

"Oh, yes; there is no doubt of that," said Mr. McGregor; "I am perfectly familiar with his signature, and there is no question in my mind but that he signed that himself."

"Well, gentlemen, I will now make up a possible case, and you can see how nearly it compares with the present matter. I will suppose that a man of wealth, refinement, and position, should become cramped for money to supply present necessities; he is intimate with the officers of a wealthy bank; he goes there one evening and is admitted by his friend, the acting cashier. He explains his embarrassment, and his friend agrees to lend him the amount which he requires. The friend completes his work, puts away his books, and figures up the amount needed. The borrower has a small balance to his credit, and he gives a note for the difference. Then the teller opens the safe, brings out a roll of bills, and begins to count out the amount. The safe door is left open, and the visitor sees within the piles of bank-notes and the rouleaux of gold. A fortune in cash is within his grasp with only a human life standing in his way; his perplexities and embarrassments come upon him with added force as he sees the means before him by which he may escape their power to annoy him. Like Tantalus, dying of thirst with the water at his very lips, this man gazes on the wealth piled up in that safe. Glancing around, he sees his friend slowly counting the paltry hundreds he is to receive; close by lies a heavy weapon, heretofore used for innocent business purposes; another glance into the safe and insanity is upon him; his brain is a perfect hell of contending passions; again the thought flashes into his mind—'Only a life between me and that money.' He seizes the heavy hammer and deals his victim a terrible blow behind the ear; as the latter falls lifeless, the murderer strikes him twice more to make sure that there shall be no witnesses to testify in the case. The deed is done, and there remains nothing to prevent him from seizing the contents of the safe. But first, he must protect himself from the danger of discovery; to this end he carefully removes his bloody clothing, gathers every vestige of paper within sight, and breaks up the waste paper baskets for fuel. He needs more flame, however, and he takes several packages of old papers to make the fire fiercer; then his eye falls on a slip of paper lying on the desk, and he twists it nervously into a lighter to convey fire from the lamp to the mass of material in the fire-place. The flame is started, and soon the clothes are reduced to ashes. Stealthily he packs the packages of bills and the rolls of coin, and when he has taken as much as he can carry, he slips noiselessly away, leaving no trace of his identity. No one has seen him enter or depart; his position is far above the reach of suspicion; every clue has been destroyed in the fire-place, and no witness to his guilt can possibly be raised up. So he thinks; and as month after month passes, as detective after detective abandons the case in despair, as the excitement dies out in the public mind, and as the friends of the deceased apparently give up the hopeless task of seeking for the murderer, his confidence becomes complete, and he no longer fears detection.

"But stop! when his victim fell a bloody corpse at his feet, *was* every witness destroyed? No, gentlemen; helpless and lifeless as that body fell, it yet had the power to avenge itself. The right hand convulsively grasps a bank note, and it is hidden from sight by the position assumed in falling; a slip of white paper dotted with figures at random, is also covered, and is quickly saturated with blood; a fragment of paper is found below the grate, twisted so tightly as to have burned only in part; lastly, the direction of the blood-spirts show that the first blow was struck on the left side. Now, gentlemen, do you think you can read the testimony of these dumb witnesses?"

"My God! I do not know what to think," said Mr. Gordon.

"I see where your suspicions lead," said Mr. Bannatine, "but I do not yet fully know whether I can see the evidence in the same light that you do. Please go on and tell us all you suspect, and your reasons."

"Yes, Mr. Pinkerton," said Mr. McGregor, "whom do you suspect?"

"Gentlemen," I replied, solemnly, "I have formed no hasty conclusion in this matter, and I should not accuse any man without the strongest reasons for believing him guilty; but I think that when I have connected together the links which I have gathered, you will agree with me in the moral certainty that George Gordon was murdered by Alexander P. Drysdale, and no other."

"Go on, go on, Mr. Pinkerton," said Mr. Gordon, in great excitement. "It seems impossible, yet there are some slight fancies in my mind which seem to confirm that theory. Tell us all your conclusions, and how you have arrived at them."

"Well, first, I am satisfied that only a particular friend would have been admitted to the bank by George that night; second, the blow was struck from behind, on the left side, showing that the murderer was probably left-handed. Mr. Drysdale satisfies both of these conditions; I visited him to-day and saw him write an address in my note-book with his left hand. Third, I have here a note for $927.78, signed 'Alexander P. Drysdale;' the signature, you say, is genuine, and further, you told me yesterday that you had not held a note of Mr. Drysdale's for some years. On reflection you will see that this note could not have been taken from the packages of bank archives which were burned, for it never could have been put there; moreover it is dated '1856,' and must have been made some time last year. As you have no record of such a note, I infer that it was drawn the night of the murder. Fourthly, I have conclusive evidence of that fact in this slip of blood-stained paper," and so saying, I produced the slip upon which George had done his figuring.

"How! where!" exclaimed my listeners.

"Near the bottom of that paper you will find in light pencil marks three numbers arranged like an example in subtraction, while the rest are all additions in ink. The figures are: first, 1,252.00; then, 324.22; and 927.78 below the line. Mr. Drysdale's balance was $324.22, and the amount of this note bearing his signature is $927.78. It looks to me as if he wanted to draw $1,252.00, and that George subtracted the amount of his balance in bank, $324.22, from the amount he wished to draw, $1,252.00, and that Mr. Drysdale then gave his note for the difference, $927.78. What do you think of my witness, gentlemen?"

The three gentlemen put their heads together over the paper long enough to convince themselves that the figures were really there, and then they resumed their seats in silence. I had watched their faces carefully as I drew my conclusions, and had seen their expressions change from incredulity to uncertainty, then to amazement, finally turning gradually to half belief; but when they sat down, positive conviction was evident in every face.

"How is it possible that these facts were never discovered before?" ejaculated Mr. Bannatine.

"It is very simple," I replied; "the search has hitherto been conducted on a wrong basis. The whole endeavor seems to have been to *guess* who might have done the deed, and then to find evidence to convict him. My plan in all similar cases is, to first examine the evidence before me, with a perfectly unbiased mind; then, having formed a theory by reasoning on general principles, as applied to the facts in my possession, I proceed to look about for some person who will answer the conditions of my theory. I may find more than one, and I then am obliged to make each such person the object of my attention until I obtain convincing proof of his innocence or guilt. The person upon whom my theory causes suspicion to fall, may have been hitherto regarded as above suspicion; but, that fact does not deter me in the least degree from placing that person's circumstances, motives, and actions under the microscope, so to speak; for experience and observation, have taught me that the most difficult crimes to fix upon the criminal, are those which have been committed by men whose previous reputation had been unspotted. Now, you have never connected Mr. Drysdale with this affair, because it has never entered your minds to suspect him; but, had you gone over the ground in the same manner that I have done, you would have been led to the same conclusion. This is the real point, where the services of an experienced detective, are most valuable. The plan by which a detective operation is to be conducted, is as important as the method of procedure. To find a man who is hiding from justice, his criminality being well known, is a task of little difficulty, compared with the labor involved in mysterious cases, where there is apparently, nothing left to identify the criminal. I claim no special credit in this case, since the clues have proven more numerous than had been supposed, but I have given you my idea of the proper way to conduct an investigation, simply to show you how I am accustomed to work. Let me now ask, whether any of you have doubts, as to the propriety of putting my detectives upon the trail of Mr. Drysdale, to determine the extent of his connection, if any, in the murder of George Gordon?"

"None whatever," said Mr. Bannatine, emphatically; "it seems almost impossible that he should be guilty; but, in the face of the strong array of accusing circumstances cited by you, Mr. Pinkerton, I can only say: 'Go on with your work in your own way.' The innocent have nothing to fear, and the guilty deserve no mercy."

"Amen," said both the other gentlemen.

"What is your plan?" asked Mr. Gordon.

"Well, gentlemen," I replied, "I have been struck with some strong points of resemblance between Drysdale and one of Bulwer's characters, Eugene Aram. You are aware, that the only evidence we can bring against Drysdale, is circumstantial, and that we could hardly obtain an indictment on the strength of it; still less a conviction for murder. Besides, there is a large amount of money at stake, and it is desirable to recover that money, as well as to convict the murderer. We must proceed, therefore, with great caution, lest we defeat our own plans by premature action. I have arranged a scheme to obtain a direct proof of Drysdale's guilt, and with your consent, I will put it in operation immediately."

I then gave the details of my plan, and the gentlemen, though somewhat nervous as to the result, finally acquiesced in it.

The next morning, I left Atkinson, for Chicago, where I duly arrived, somewhat improved in health, by my Southern trip. I immediately sent for Timothy Webster, one of my most expert detectives, to whom I gave full charge of the case in Atkinson. I explained to him all the circumstances connected with it, and instructed him in the plan I had arranged. Mrs. Kate Warne, and a young man named Green, were assigned to assist Webster, and all the necessary disguises and clothing, were prepared at short notice.

Mrs. Warne was the first lady whom I had ever employed, and this was one of the earliest operations in which she was engaged. As a detective, she had no superior, and she was a lady of such refinement, tact, and discretion, that I never hesitated to entrust to her some of my most difficult undertakings.

It will be understood by the reader, that each detective made daily reports to me, and that I constantly directed the operation by mail or telegraph. This has always been my invariable custom, and no important steps are ever taken without my order, unless circumstances should occur which would not admit the delay.

CHAPTER IV.

ABOUT a week after my departure from Atkinson, a gentleman arrived there by the evening train, and went to the hotel. He was an intelligent, shrewd, agreeable business man, about thirty-five years old, and he impressed all who made his acquaintance, as a gentleman of ability and energy. He signed the register, as 'John M. Andrews, Baltimore,' and the landlord soon learned from him that he had come to Atkinson to reside permanently, if he could get into business there. Mr. Andrews was evidently a man of considerable wealth, though he made no ostentatious display, nor did he talk about his property as though he cared to impress upon other people the idea that he was rich. Still, it came to be generally understood, in a few days, that he had made quite a fortune, as a cotton broker, in Baltimore, and that he had a considerable sum in cash to invest, when a desirable opportunity should offer. This fact, together with his agreeable manners, made his society quite an acquisition to the town, and he was soon on familiar terms with all the regular boarders in the hotel, and with many prominent residents of the place.

Some days after Mr. Andrews arrived the hotel received another equally popular guest. She gave her name, as Mrs. R. C. Potter, and her object in visiting Atkinson, was to improve her health. She was accompanied by her father, Mr. C. B. Rowell, a fine looking, white-haired old gentleman, but he remained only long enough to see her comfortably settled, and then returned to their home in Jacksonville, Florida, as his business required his immediate presence there. Mrs. Potter was a distingushed looking brunette; she was a widow with no children, and she might have passed for thirty years of age. She was tall and graceful, and her entertaining conversation made her a general favorite among the ladies in the hotel. She was not an invalid, strictly speaking, but the family physician had recommended that she should go to the dry air of northern Mississippi for a few months, to escape the rainy, foggy weather of Florida at that season.

About a week after her arrival, she went out with two other ladies, Mrs. Townsend and Mrs. Richter, to explore the beauties of Rocky Creek. They spent a pleasant afternoon in the wooded ravines, and it was after five o'clock, before they returned. As they sauntered down one of the pleasantest streets of the town, they noticed a lady standing at the gate of an elegant residence, with large grounds.

"Oh! there is Mrs. Drysdale," said Mrs Townsend. " Have you met her, Mrs. Potter?"

"Not yet, though I have heard of her so frequently, that I feel almost as if I knew her."

"Well, I think you will like each other very much," said Mrs. Richter, " and we will introduce you to her."

On reaching the gate, therefore, the ladies presented Mrs. Potter in due form.

"I have been intending to call on you, Mrs. Potter,"

said Mrs. Drysdale, "but my youngest child has not been well, and I have not gone anywhere for several weeks. In fact, I am quite a home body at all times, and I always expect my friends to waive ceremony, and visit me a great deal more than I visit them. I hope you will not wait for me, Mrs. Potter, for my domestic affairs keep me very busy just now; I shall be glad to see you any time that you feel like dropping in."

"I shall be very glad to dispense with formalities," answered Mrs. Potter, "and you can depend upon seeing me soon."

After some further conversation, the three ladies resumed their homeward walk, leaving Mrs. Drysdale still waiting for her husband. He was soon seen by the ladies, rapidly walking up the street toward his home. He was on the opposite side, so that he merely bowed to them, and hastened on.

"There seems to have been quite a change in Mr. Drysdale during the last year," said Mrs. Richter. "My husband was speaking of it the other day. He said that Drysdale was becoming really unsociable. I hope he is not growing dissipated, for the sake of his wife, who is a lovely woman."

"Yes; she seems to be a most devoted wife and mother," said Mrs. Potter. "Possibly, the change in Mr. Drysdale, is due to business troubles."

"Oh, no; that is impossible," said Mrs. Townsend; "he is very wealthy indeed, and as he is not engaged in any regular business, he cannot be financially embarrassed. No, I attribute his recent peculiarities, to religious doubts; he has not been to church since last fall."

"Is it as long as that?" asked Mrs. Richter.

"Yes; I recollect it, because he did not go to the funeral of poor George Gordon, and he has not attended service since then."

"Well, if he really is in religious trouble, the minister ought to visit him and give him advice," said Mrs. Richter.

As they walked toward the hotel, they turned the conversation into a different channel without reaching any conclusion as to the cause of Mr. Drysdale's eccentricities.

A few days thereafter Mrs. Potter called upon Mrs. Drysdale and passed the afternoon very pleasantly. When Mr. Drysdale came home he was very polite and agreeable; he seemed glad to find his wife enjoying herself, and when Mrs. Potter rose to go, both husband and wife urged her warmly to come frequently.

"I am going out to my plantation in a day or two," said Mr. Drysdale, "and I hope you will visit my wife while I am gone, as I am afraid she may be lonesome."

"Who are you going with?" asked Mrs. Drysdale.

"There is a gentleman from Baltimore, staying at the hotel," replied Mr. Drysdale, "and he talks of investing some money in land, so I thought I would take him out to see Bristed's old place next to mine. It is going to ruin now, but if a man like Mr. Andrews would take it, he could make it pay. He seems very intelligent and agreeable; I suppose you have met him, Mrs. Potter?"

"Oh, yes; he was introduced to me the first week I was here," replied Mrs. Potter. "He seems to me to be a Southern gentleman with a good deal of real Yankee shrewdness."

"That is my opinion, also," said Mr. Drysdale, "and if he buys Bristed's place, he will join me in some improvements which are much needed."

"Well, good afternoon, Mrs. Drysdale," said Mrs. Potter; "I am going out horseback riding in a day or two, and perhaps I will stop here a few minutes on my way back."

"Do so, Mrs. Potter; we shall be delighted to see you. Good afternoon."

On Mrs. Potter's return to the hotel, she stayed in the parlor for some time, and as Mr. Andrews came in soon after, they had a pleasant *tete-a-tete* before going to dinner.

The next morning Mr. Andrews went out to get a cabinet-maker to make a small book-case for his room, and the hotel clerk directed him to the shop of Mr. Breed. The latter said that he was very busy, indeed, but that he could get a young man who was boarding with him to do the job.

"Is he a good workman?" asked Mr. Andrews.

"I think he is," replied Breed, "though I am not sure, as he came here only day before yesterday from Memphis. He has served his time at the trade, however, and he ought to be able to make a book-case neatly."

"Well, send him over, Mr. Breed, and I will give him a trial. By the way, who was that gentleman that just passed? I have seen him several times, but have never met him in society."

"That was Mr. Peter A. Gordon," said Breed. "He boards at the hotel, also, but he rarely mingles with other men except in business."

"I am surprised at that," Mr. Andrews remarked, "for

he appears like a naturally genial man; yet he has a very sad look."

"Yes; he has never recovered from the shock of his nephew's murder last fall; he always used to be very sociable and hospitable, but now he seems too much cast down to care for society. You may have heard of the dreadful manner in which young George Gordon was murdered?"

"Oh, yes; I recollect," said Mr. Andrews; "the circumstances were related to me soon after I arrived here. George Gordon seems to have been a fine young fellow, and I don't wonder the old gentleman mourns his loss."

"He was one of the most promising young men I ever knew," said Mr. Breed, warmly; "and speaking of poor George, reminds me that I noticed a strong resemblance to him in this young workman boarding with me. Ordinarily I would not have perceived it, but yesterday he slipped on a coat of mine, which was just like the one George used to wear, and the likeness was remarkable."

"You were one of the first at the bank the day after the murder, were you not, Mr. Breed?"

"Yes; and it was a dreadful sight. It was wonderful how Mr. Peter Gordon retained his presence of mind; he did not break down until he found that there was no hope of discovering the murderer."

"Was no one ever suspected?" asked Mr. Andrews.

"Oh, yes; several persons were arrested—gamblers and loafers—but they all proved their innocence conclusively."

Mr. Andrews showed considerable interest in the

murder, and Mr. Breed related all that was known about it. When he was about to go, Mr. Andrews said :

"Well, it is a very mysterious affair, and I am not surprised that Mr. Gordon is so dejected; that horrible scene must be always before him. By the way, don't let your young man dress in gray, when he comes to my room; I should be continually haunted with a suspicion that it was a ghost."

"Please don't speak of that to any one," said Mr. Breed, confidentially; "I ought not to have mentioned it myself, for young Green was frightened nearly out of his wits about it. As I said before, when he wears his every-day clothes, no one would notice any special resemblance, but in that particular style of dress, the likeness was really alarming. He was so scared, that in future, he will take great care not to be seen in any clothes like those of poor George."

"Of course, I shall not mention the matter," said Mr. Andrews; "send him over this afternoon."

CHAPTER V.

ON leaving Mr. Breed, Mr. Andrews paid a visit to Mr. Drysdale, at the latter's office.

"I hope I shall not interfere with your work, Mr. Drysdale," he said. "I am an idler for the present, but I try to respect the business hours of others, and so, if I disturb you, let me know it."

"Oh! not at all, I assure you," said Mr. Drysdale, warmly. "I am never very busy, and just now, there is nothing whatever to do. Indeed, I wish I had more to do—this lack of steady work wears upon me. I need something to keep my mind constantly occupied."

"That is where you and I differ," said Andrews; "I have worked pretty hard for twenty years, and now I am willing to take a rest. I don't wish to be wholly idle, but I like to give up a good part of my time to recreation."

"I used to feel so, too," said Drysdale, as if his thoughts were far away; then, he added, hastily, as if recollecting himself: "I mean that I have felt so at times, but I always need to come back to hard work again. Will you be ready to go out to my plantation next Monday?"

"Yes; Monday will suit me as well as any other day," replied Andrews. "When shall we return?"

"I had not intended to remain there more than three

or four days, unless you should wish to stay longer. If agreeable to you, we will return Thursday afternoon."

"That will enable me to join our riding party the next day," said Andrews. "All right; I will be ready to start Monday morning. Now, I must be going; I only stopped to find out when you would be ready to go."

"I am sorry you cannot stay longer," said Drysdale. "I hope that you will drop in without ceremony, whenever you feel like it."

In the afternoon, young Green, the cabinet-maker, called upon Mr. Andrews, and went up to the latter's room. The work to be done, must have required a great deal of explanation, as Green remained nearly an hour. As he went out, Mr. Andrews said to him:

"If we fail to return Thursday, you must be there Friday at the same hour. You had better take a look at the place before then."

On Monday, Mr. Drysdale called at the hotel immediately after breakfast, and found Mr. Andrews all ready for the ride to the plantation. As they rode out of town, Mr. Drysdale's spirits seemed to rise rapidly, and he entertained his companion so successfully, that when they reached the plantation, they had become quite well acquainted with each other. Drysdale was a man of fine education, and fascinating manners; he really had great eloquence, and his abilities were far above the average, but the circumstances of his life had not been such as to develop his powers, and give play to his ambition; hence, he was apparently becoming disappointed, sour, and morose. At least, this was the impression which many of his friends had gained, and they accounted for the gradual change in his manners on the above theory; namely, that he was the victim of disappointed ambition.

During their stay at the plantation, the gentlemen usually spent their evenings together, while the mornings were given up to business by Drysdale, and to hunting by Andrews. The plantation required a great deal of attention just in the spring, and Drysdale's time was pretty well occupied. Andrews easily formed the acquaintance of the neighboring planters, and he spent much of his time in paying visits around the country. He thought quite favorably of buying the Bristed plantation, as Drysdale had hoped, but the owner wished to sell another place with it, and Andrews did not care to buy both. Drysdale suggested that by autumn, the owner would be willing to sell it separately, and he advised Andrews to hold off until then.

On Thursday, Andrews started out shooting early, agreeing to be back at noon, to make an early start for Atkinson, as the time required to ride there, was about four hours. He strayed so far away, however, that it was two o'clock before he returned, and they did not mount their horses until three o'clock. By this time, they had become much more intimate than one would have expected on so short acquaintance, and Drysdale showed a marked pleasure in the company of his new friend. During the first part of the ride, he was as brilliant and entertaining as possible, but, as they approached the town, he began to lose his cheerfulness, and to become almost gloomy. Both gentlemen were rather tired, and they soon allowed the conversation to drop almost wholly.

It was early dusk when they reached the banks of Rocky Creek, about a mile from Drysdale's house. From this point, the scenery was bold and picturesque; the road passed through heavy masses of timber at times, and crossed many ravines and rocky gorges, as it followed the general direction of the winding stream. Daylight was rapidly fading into the night, though objects could still be distinguished quite well at a distance of one hundred yards. As they arrived at one of the wooded hillocks, over which the road passed, they were shut out from any very extended view, except in one direction. Here, Andrews reined in his horse a moment, to take a last look at the beauty of the scene, while Drysdale passed on a few yards in advance.

The spot was rather wild and perhaps a little weird; on the right was a dense forest, rising some distance above the road, which curved around the hill-side about mid-way to the crest; on the left the hill descended rapidly to the creek, along which ran a heavy belt of timber, which permitted only an occasional gleam of water to be seen; the abrupt hill-side between the road and the timber was nearly cleared of undergrowth, but it was filled with large boulders and creeping vines; over the tops of the timber the country stretched away in dissolving views as the mists of night began to form and spread over the landscape. Having paused an instant, Andrews spurred his horse forward just as Drysdale uttered an exclamation of horror. As he came up, he saw that Drysdale had stopped and was holding his reins in a convulsive grasp; all color was gone from his face, and he was trembling violently.

"What is the matter, Drysdale?" said Andrews, drawing up beside him.

"My God! look there!" broke from Drysdale's ashy lips, as he pointed down the hill-side.

At the distance of about fifty yards the figure of a young man was moving down the slope toward the timber. He walked slowly on, with a measured pace, turning his eyes neither to the right nor left. He was apparently about twenty-five or twenty-six years of age, and his face was indicative of intelligence, ability and energy. His course was nearly parallel to the direction of the road at that point, and only his profile could be seen. He wore a business suit of light gray clothes, but he had no hat on his head, and his curly hair was tossed lightly by the evening breeze. As he moved further from the road, the back of his head was more directly exposed, presenting a most ghastly sight. The thick brown locks were matted together in a mass of gore, and large drops of blood slowly trickled down upon his coat; the whole back of the skull seemed to be crushed in, while the deadly pallor of his face gave him the appearance of a corpse.

Drysdale seemed to rally his faculties a moment and shouted in powerful but hoarse tones:

"Say! you, sir! Who are you, and where are you going?"

Although his voice might have been heard at a long distance, the figure continued its course without indicating, even by a sign, that he had heard the hail.

"Why, what in the devil has got into you, Drysdale?"

"'My God! look there!' broke from Drysdale's ashy lips, as he pointed down the hill-side."—Page 58.

asked Andrews. "Whom are you shouting at in such a savage way?"

"Don't you see that man down the hill?" he asked, in a perfect agony of fear and excitement. "See! right in line with that pointed rock; why, he is only a few yards off. My God! it can't be possible that you don't see him!"

"Upon my word, Drysdale," said Andrews, "if you keep on, I shall think you are going crazy. What man are you talking about? There is no one in sight, and either you are trying to play a joke on me, or else your imagination is most unpleasantly active."

"Andrews, look where I point, less than ten rods off," said Drysdale, in a hoarse whisper, clutching Andrews by the arm; "do you mean to say that you don't see a man slowly walking toward the creek?"

"I mean to say," replied Andrews, deliberately, "that there is no man in sight from here, either on that hill-side or any where else."

"God help me," muttered Drysdale, as the figure disappeared in the woods, "then it must have been a ghost."

"My dear fellow," said Andrews, sympathizingly, as they continued their ride, "I am afraid you are feverish; you probably imagined you saw something, and you are superstitious about the matter because I did not see it. Tell me what it was."

By this time they had passed some distance beyond the spot where Drysdale had seen the apparition, and he began to recover his strength somewhat. It was evident that he was still very much distressed, but he endeavored to pass the matter over.

"Oh! it was nothing of any consequence," he said, "but I thought I saw a man crossing that clearing."

"Well, what of it?" asked Andrews. "Was he a dangerous looking fellow?"

"Yes; very dangerous looking, indeed;" then, suddenly, as if struck by a plausible idea, he added: "I thought it was a negro with a gun; you know what my opinions are about allowing the slaves to have fire-arms, and this fellow looked like such a villain that I was really alarmed. You are sure you saw no one?"

"Quite sure," replied Andrews. "I am afraid you have worked too hard, and that you are going to be ill. I shall tell your wife to nurse you well for a few days to cure you of seeing spooks and wild niggers roaming 'round with guns."

"No, indeed," said Drysdale, hastily; "please say nothing to my wife; it would only alarm her unnecessarily."

"Well, take my advice and rest awhile," said Andrews. "Your nerves are a little shaken, and you will certainly be ill if you keep on working so steadily."

Drysdale soon relapsed into moody silence, and when they reached his gate, he was a really pitiable object. He asked Andrews to take supper with him, but as the invitation was given only as a matter of form, the latter excused himself, and rode immediately to the hotel. He happened to meet Mrs. Potter in the parlor, but he stopped only a few minutes to talk to her, as he was too hungry and tired to feel like entertaining the fascinating widow.

It was then only about seven o'clock, and Mrs. Potter

proposed to Mrs. Townsend, and several other ladies and gentlemen, that they take a walk. Accordingly, they strolled through the pleasant streets, enjoying the balmy spring air, and often stopping at the gates of their friends, to chat a few minutes. As they passed the Drysdale place, Mrs. Potter said:

"I want to run in to speak to Mrs. Drysdale a minute; I promised to stop here on our riding excursion to-morrow, but as it is postponed, I want to tell her not to expect me."

The rest of the party stayed at the gate, while Mrs. Potter went in. She was ushered into the library, and Mrs. Drysdale came down at once. Having explained her object in calling, Mrs. Potter asked whether Mr. and Mrs. Drysdale would not join the party outside, for a short walk.

"I am sorry to say, that my husband is quite unwell," said Mrs. Drysdale. "He returned from the plantation to-day, quite feverish, and excited, and now he is in a sort of nervous delirium. He has had one or two attacks before, but none so serious as this."

"I sincerely hope he is not going to be ill," said Mrs. Potter. "What does the doctor think?"

"Oh! he won't have a doctor," replied Mrs. Drysdale; "he says that I am the best doctor he can have, because I can soothe him."

Just then, Mrs. Potter heard a heavy footstep, beginning to pace up and down overhead.

"There, he has arisen,' said Mrs. Drysdale, "and I shall find him pacing the room, and muttering to himself like a crazy man. You must excuse me, as I must go to quiet him."

"Oh, certainly; I am sorry I called you away. Please let me know if I can do anything for you. If Mr. Drysdale should be seriously ill, don't be afraid to call upon me. I am an excellent nurse, and nothing would give me greater pleasure than to assist you; or, at least, I could look after the children."

"You are very kind, Mrs. Potter, and I shall be glad to accept your assistance, especially, as the children are so fond of you; however, I hope Aleck's illness will be only temporary."

Mrs. Potter then withdrew, and the party slowly strolled back to the hotel.

As Mrs. Drysdale surmised, her husband's illness was very brief, and in two or three days, he returned to his duties at the court house. He was somewhat changed in looks, however, his face being haggard, his figure slightly bowed, and his hand tremulous. He seemed, more than ever before, to avoid society, and on his way to the court house, he always chose the least frequented streets. The change in his looks and manners, was noticed only by a few who had formerly been intimate with him; in this little circle, his eccentricities were accounted for by significant gestures of drinking, and it was understood among those who knew him best, that liquor was responsible for the ruin of another fine fellow.

One peculiarity that he evinced was, a great partiality for the society of Mr. Andrews, and for the next week, they were together every day. He frequently referred, in conversation with Andrews, to the freak his imagination had played, while returning from the plantation, and, though Andrews always made light of it, and laughed at him, he evidently thought about it a great deal. It seemed to be a kind of relief to him to discuss it with Andrews, and so the latter used to humor him in it.

CHAPTER VI.

SEVERAL days after Drysdale's return from the plantation, Mrs. Potter and several others, set out for a horseback ride. They enjoyed the afternoon exceedingly, and it was growing dark before they reached the town on their return. As the party passed down the street upon which Drysdale lived, Mrs. Potter, and another lady, lagged behind the others, and the main body were quite a distance in advance. Mrs. Potter suggested that they put their horses at full speed, in order to overtake their friends. Mrs. Robbins, her companion, assented, and they dashed off together. The latter's horse was the faster of the two, however, and Mrs. Potter was about fifty or sixty yards in the rear, when they approached the Drysdale place. There was no one in sight on the street, and there was so much foliage on each side, that the road was quite hidden from the view of the scattered houses.

Suddenly, Mrs. Robbins heard a shriek and a fall behind her; quickly reining in her horse, she turned back, passing Mrs. Potter's riderless horse on the way. She soon discovered Mrs. Potter lying by the roadside, groaning, and in great pain. Mrs. Robbins did not stop to ask any questions; she saw that Mrs. Potter was badly hurt, and she knew that assistance must be brought instantly. She therefore, galloped up the drive to the

"She soon discovered Mrs. Potter lying by the road-side, groaning and in great pain."—Page 64.

Drysdale house, and hastily told them what had happened. In less than three minutes, Mr. Drysdale had improvised a stretcher out of a wicker settee and a mattress, and had summoned four stout negroes to bring it after him, while he and his wife hurried out to the road. There they found Mrs. Potter, and Mrs. Robbins supporting her. She said that she was in great pain, from severe contusion, and possible dislocation of the knee joint, and that she had also sustained some internal injuries. In a very few minutes, they had tenderly placed her on the settee, and carried her up to the house. She was carefully put to bed, and Mrs. Robbins remounted her horse to go for a physician. The latter, on his arrival, said that he could hardly tell the extent of Mrs. Potter's injuries at once, but he thought they would not confine her to her bed more than a week or two. She asked if she might be moved to the hotel, as she did not wish to trespass on Mrs. Drysdale's hospitality. Mrs. Drysdale, however, refused to hear of such a thing as the removal of a sick person from her house, and she said that she should enjoy Mrs. Potter's society enough to compensate for the slight trouble. It was decided, therefore, that Mrs. Potter should remain until she was able to go without assistance. She improved very rapidly, but her knee seemed to pain her considerably, and she spent most of her time in her room, or on a sofa under the veranda, whither her stout negro nurse used to carry her.

A few days afterwards, Mrs. Potter was lying awake in her room at about seven o'clock in the morning. Mr. and Mrs. Drysdale's room was next to hers, and the transom over the connecting door was open, so that whatever was said in one room could be easily heard in the other. Mrs. Potter heard Drysdale get up and open the blinds to let in the morning sun. He had hardly done so ere he gave a sharp cry and sank into a chair.

"What is the matter?" asked Mrs. Drysdale, in great alarm.

"Oh, nothing," he replied; "I don't feel well."

"I should think you wouldn't," said Mrs. Drysdale, "for you have had the nose-bleed terribly. Why, it is all over the pillow and floor, and leads out of the door. You must have gone down stairs."

"Yes, yes," he exclaimed, hastily, "I did get up in the night. I—I don't feel very well—I guess I will lie down again."

"Is there anything I can do for you?" asked his wife, anxiously.

"No, nothing at present. Just go right along with your household affairs, as usual; I shall be all right in a short time."

Mrs. Drysdale saw that her husband was nervous and irritable, and so she dressed quickly and went down to superintend her domestic duties. When Mrs. Potter's breakfast was ready, she brought it up herself and stopped a few minutes to talk.

"Do you know of any remedy for bleeding at the nose, Mrs. Potter?" she asked. "My husband had quite a severe attack last night, and he went down on the front veranda, and then down the gravel walk, thinking, I suppose, that exercise would stop it. It must have bled frightfully, for I could see marks of blood all the way down the path to the gate."

"I suppose he let it run instead of trying to stop the flow," replied Mrs. Potter. "Some people think it is good for the health occasionally, and so they allow the nose to bleed as long as it wants to."

After a few more remarks, Mrs. Drysdale went down stairs again. Mrs. Potter could hear Mr. Drysdale tossing about on the bed in the next room, muttering to himself, and occasionally speaking aloud such expressions as — "Oh! this is horrible!" — "What does this mean?" — "My God! what could have done it?"

After a time he became quieter, but he did not leave his room until the afternoon. Soon after he got up, Mr. Andrews called to see him, having failed to find him at his office.

"I thought you might be sick and so I dropped in to see you," he said.

"I am very glad you came," replied Drysdale. "I have been a little unwell, and I need some one to cheer me up."

"Let us take a short walk," said Andrews; "the exercise will do you good."

As they strolled out, Andrews pointed to some blood and said:

"Any one hurt in your house?"

"No—yes—that is, nothing serious; one of my negroes cut his hand this morning," replied Drysdale, shuddering. "I can't look at blood without feeling sick," he explained, as he saw that Andrews was wondering at his agitation.

As they continued their walk, Andrews noticed that

Drysdale was very self-absorbed, and so they strolled down the street without conversing. Their course took them past the bank, and as Mr. McGregor was standing on the steps of the side entrance, he accosted them heartily.

"Why, how do you do, gentlemen?" he asked. "Won't you walk in for a few minutes? I havn't seen you since your illness, Mr. Drysdale; won't you come in and rest a while?"

On hearing McGregor's salutation, Drysdale started as if stung, and trembled violently. He had been walking along with his eyes down, so that he had not seen Mr. McGregor until spoken to.

"No, thank you," he replied; "I think I won't have time—that is, I promised my wife to come back soon. You must excuse me this time."

He hurried on with a nervous gesture of courtesy, and he did not recover his calmness until some minutes afterward. Andrews accompanied him to his home, and on the way they agreed to go to Drysdale's plantation for a short visit on the following Monday. Having settled upon the time for starting and returning, Andrews declined an invitation to dine with Drysdale that evening, and they separated. Andrews dropped into Breed's shop on his way back to the hotel, and there he found young Green, the man who had made his book-case. They talked together only a few minutes, and Andrews then went to his room, where he stayed the remainder of the day.

On Monday, Andrews and Drysdale rode off to the plantation at daylight, and the latter's spirits seemed to lighten rapidly after leaving the immediate vicinity of Atkinson. In the afternoon, Andrews took his gun and wandered off into the woods, but he did not seem very desirous of shooting anything, for he soon took a position whence he commanded a full view of the house. In about half an hour, Drysdale came out and walked slowly toward a small cluster of trees, about five hundred yards from the house. Here, he leaned against a tree, and paused to look around in every direction; then he began to stride with a measured step in a straight line. When he stopped, he began to examine the ground carefully for some minutes, and finally, he seemed satisfied with his inspection, and returned to the house.

During the remainder of their stay at the plantation, Andrews and Drysdale were constantly together, and the latter seemed to find the greatest pleasure in the former's society. He frequently recurred to the subject of ghosts and spooks, and always closed by discussing the character of the apparition he had seen on the roadside. There was no doubt that it had made a deep impression upon him, for he never tired of talking about it. Andrews laughed at him, ridiculed his vivid imagination, cross-questioned him, and reasoned with him upon the absurdity of his hallucination, but all to no effect; Drysdale maintained in the most dogged manner, that he had seen a ghost.

On Friday, they were to return to Atkinson, and in the morning Andrews rode over to make a short visit to a neighbor. He was so hospitably entertained, however, that he did not get away until after two o'clock, and it was nearly three before they started on their homeward ride. As before, it was growing dusky, when they reached the banks of Rocky Creek, and Drysdale was in a state of high nervous excitement.

On reaching the spot where Drysdale had seen the ghost before, he kept close at Andrews' side, and endeavored to appear unconcerned. Suddenly, he grasped Andrews by the arm with a faint groan, and said:

"Andrews, look! look! for God's sake, tell me, don't you see it?"

As he spoke, he pointed toward the same ghastly object which he had seen before. There, right under his eyes, passed the image of the murdered George Gordon.

"There, I was afraid you would have the same folly again," said Andrews, soothingly, as if anxious to attract his attention away from his ghostly friend. "What the devil is the matter with you?"

"Tell me, tell me, Andrews," gasped Drysdale, in such terror that his parched throat and quivering lips could hardly pronounce the words; "can't you see that horrible man close to the fence, walking toward the creek?"

"I tell you, my dear fellow," replied Andrews, earnestly, "that you are laboring under a most unpleasant hallucination. There is absolutely no person, or any moving object in sight, except you and me."

At this moment, the sound of approaching hoof-beats could be plainly heard, and Drysdale turned his head to look back in the direction whence they came. On looking for the ghost again, it was nowhere to be seen.

"Andrews, it is gone—the earth has swallowed it up," he said.

He would have fallen from his horse, if Andrews had

not caught him around the waist, and just as he did so, Mr. Breed and Mr. O'Fallon, the station agent, rode up, one on each side of them.

"What's the matter with Mr. Drysdale?" asked O'Fallon.

"Didn't you see it? Tell me—did the ghost pass you?" Drysdale queried eagerly, turning toward the new comers.

"What are you talking about? What do you mean by 'the ghost?'" asked Mr. Breed, in great wonderment.

"The ghost, I say—did neither of you see a horrible figure pass out of sight suddenly, toward the creek yonder?"

"I saw nothing, Mr. Drysdale," said O'Fallon; "did you, Breed?"

"Well, I don't know what Mr. Drysdale means by a ghost," said Breed, deliberately; "but I think I did see something down there. I couldn't say what it looked like. Why do you call it a ghost, Mr. Drysdale?"

"Because I have seen it twice close to me, and Mr. Andrews has not been able to see it at all," replied Drysdale with great difficulty. "I began to think it must have been imagination on my part, but now, that you have seen it, I know that it was a ghost."

Drysdale was so helpless, that it was necessary for one gentleman to ride on each side of him to hold him in his saddle. On arriving at his place, they helped him into the house, and left him in charge of his wife. He immediately went to bed, and during the night, he suffered a great deal. Mrs. Potter heard him groaning, tossing, and muttering until nearly daylight.

The story of the ghost was soon freely circulated by

O'Fallon and Breed, though they could not describe the apparition at all. Still, it created quite an excitement, and the results were not very beneficial to the neighborhood, for the reason that no negro could be induced to pass along that part of the road after dark; indeed, there were a great many educated white people who would not ride past the spot alone on a dark night.

Drysdale was confined to his room for several days, during which time he received no visitors except Andrews. It was curious to observe what a strong preference he showed for his new-found friend.

Just at this time I decided to re-visit Atkinson myself, and on my arrival there I had a long interview with Messrs. Ballantine, McGregor, and Gordon. I explained to them all the steps I had taken, and they learned to their great astonishment that Mr. Andrews, Mrs. Potter, and Mr. Green were my detectives. The ghost was Green, whose resemblance to young Gordon was a great aid in carrying out the scheme. Mrs. Potter had voluntarily fallen from her horse in order to get herself carried into Drysdale's house, and it was she who sprinkled the blood over Drysdale's clothing and down the walk. After settling all our plans, I returned to the hotel, where I was easily able to obtain a private interview with Mr. Andrews and Mr. Green.

I gave full instructions to Andrews, and he informed Mrs. Potter of my wishes, at the same time conveying to her another large bottle of blood.

CHAPTER VII.

ABOUT one o'clock that night Mrs. Potter rose, quietly dressed herself, and stealthily left the house. She walked to the nearest point on the creek and began to drop blood from her bottle. She spilled small portions of it all the way back to the house, up the front walk, in the hall, and finally, slipping into Drysdale's room, she scattered the crimson drops on his pillow. She then retired to bed.

When she awoke in the morning, she found Mrs. Drysdale in a very uneasy state of mind. She said that her husband had again been attacked by bleeding at the nose, and that he was quite weak from the loss of blood. Mrs. Potter deeply sympathized with Mrs. Drysdale, but she could assist her only by kind and consoling words.

The family had hardly finished their breakfast when a number of the neighbors came in in a high state of excitement. They said that blood had been discovered on the grass near where the ghost had been seen, and that quite a crowd had gathered around it. They had found other blood-marks at intervals along the road, and on following the direction in which they traveled, it was found that they led straight to Drysdale's house. The question now arose, did the wounded person go from the house to the creek, or *vice versa*. Drysdale was terribly excited on learning of the discovery, and he was soon in a species of delirium. It was known that he was quite sick, so that the neighbors soon withdrew. Many thought that the blood was that of a burglar or negro sneak-thief, who might have gone to Drysdale's house to steal, but who had been frightened off before he had secured any plunder. The blood might have been from an old hurt. Others, more superstitiously inclined, believed that the ghost was in some way responsible for the blood. No one was able to solve the mystery, however, and it added to the terror with which the ghost story had inspired the negroes.

Drysdale was now confined to his bed, and he would see no one except his wife and Andrews. He insisted that he was not sick, but only run down by overwork, and so refused to have a doctor. Andrews' influence over him was greater than that of any one else, and it was plain that the latter had completely secured his confidence. As I now felt convinced that Drysdale would surely confess in a short time, I returned to Chicago, leaving the whole charge of the operation with Andrews.

A few nights later Mrs. Potter was troubled with the tooth-ache, and she lay awake most of the night. Suddenly she heard footsteps in Drysdale's room, and then she saw Drysdale pass her window on the veranda. He was dressed in slippers and night-dress, and his actions were so strange that she determined to follow him. Hastily putting on some dark clothes, she hurried cautiously after him. The night was clear with no moon, and she was able to distinguish his white figure at a considerable distance. He walked rapidly to the creek and followed its windings a short distance; then he paused a few minutes, as if reflecting. This enabled Mrs. Potter to hide herself near by in some undergrowth, whence she could watch him more carefully. To her great astonishment, she saw him walk into the creek at a shallow spot, and begin wading up against the current. Very soon he stopped and leaned over with his hands in the water, as if he were feeling for something. In a few minutes he came out of the stream, on the opposite side from that on which he had entered, and took a path to a foot-bridge leading across the creek toward his house. As soon as she saw that he was on his way back, she hastened home as rapidly as possible, arriving there only a few seconds before him.

The next morning, Drysdale appeared at the breakfast table for the first time, in several days. He remarked that he felt much better, but he said nothing of his midnight walk, nor did his wife, as she had slept in a separate room; however, she was probably ignorant of it.

Neither Mrs. Potter, nor Mr. Andrews could imagine what Drysdale's object was in making his pilgrimage to the creek at that time of night, especially as he had always shown the greatest aversion to that vicinity, ever since he had first seen the ghost. I was equally puzzled when I was informed of his freak, but I determined to make use of the incident, in case he should do the same thing again. I therefore instructed Andrews to have Green watch the house every night, dressed in his apparition suit. He was then to "shadow" Drysdale, when the latter went out, and if a favorable opportunity should present itself, he was to appear before him in full view in the role of the ghost.

By this time, Drysdale had recovered sufficiently, to attend to his office duties, but he always seemed anxious to have Andrews with him. Andrews had talked very encouragingly to him, showing a good deal of sympathy, and thus, they had become quite confidential friends. He, therefore, assured Drysdale that he should be happy to give him as much of his company, as possible, if it would afford Drysdale any pleasure.

"You are very kind, Mr. Andrews," said Drysdale; "you may think it strange, but I feel a sense of relief, when I am with you, especially lately. I wonder if I shall ever be better," he mused plaintively.

"Why, certainly; we hope for your speedy recovery," said Andrews, cheerfully. "You let trivial matters prey on your mind, and you must stop it, for your health will not stand it."

"Well, I shall try," responded Drysdale feebly.

One evening, Mrs. Drysdale was sitting at Mrs. Potter's side, waiting for her husband's return. By this time, Mrs. Potter was able to sit up, and even to move about the room somewhat.

"My husband is failing in health, I fear," said Mrs. Drysdale.

"I am afraid so, too," replied Mrs. Potter, "and I feel sorry to think that I am a burden upon you at the same time; but, I hope to be well soon, and then I will help you take care of him."

"You have been no burden whatever, Mrs. Potter; on the contrary, your company has been a great comfort to me.' But, I was thinking, that if my husband would try a change of air and life, it would be a great help to him. I should miss him sadly, but I would make any sacrifice to see him restored to health."

At the tea table, Mrs. Drysdale said:

"I was just speaking to Mrs. Potter about your health, Aleck, and I thought that if you would go away for a time, the change of scenery, and habits of life, would be very advantageous. Why don't you go down to New Orleans with Mr. Andrews? He is always talking of going there, but he is too lazy to start. You could both enjoy yourselves very much, and I know it would do you good. You would return as healthy and happy as you always used to be."

"I have been thinking of going there, or to some other place," said Drysdale, "but I can't leave just now. I think a trip would do me good, and as soon as I feel able to do so, I will get Andrews to go with me."

Nothing of interest occurred for several days. Green kept a close watch every night, but Drysdale did not appear. Andrews got Drysdale to go out hunting with him twice, but each time, Drysdale succeeded in arriving at home before dark. Green had kept up his vigils for over a week, and he began to think there was no use in them. One night, however, as he lay behind a bush, watching the house, he was suddenly aware of a white figure gliding noiselessly by him. Forewarned, though he was, the ghostly stillness with which it moved, gave him quite a severe fright, before he recollected that it was Drysdale. He immediately followed the figure and noted his every movement. In the same way, as he had done at first, he now proceeded, and after walking up the stream a short distance, he reached down, felt for something at the bottom, and then came out. As he slowly walked home, he passed within a few feet of Green, who made a considerable noise to attract his attention; but, Drysdale passed straight on, looking neither to the right nor left, and Green was unable to play ghost for the lack of an audience.

Green's account was the exact counterpart of Mrs. Potter's, and I was puzzled to account for this new move. As I sat in my office, in Chicago, with Green's report before me, the idea flashed into my mind, that possibly some of the stolen money was hidden at the bottom of the creek. Recollecting the gold pieces, which had been found on the banks of the creek, I surmised that the remainder of the gold was buried somewhere in the bed of the stream. I had no doubt of the eventual recovery of all the money, and so I decided to let that matter rest until I had complete evidence of Drysdale's guilt.

A few days after the midnight walk, Drysdale invited Andrews to make another visit to the plantation, saying,

"My overseer sends me word that he needs a great many things, and I think I had better go out to see what is wanted, myself. I would like to have you go with me, for, to tell the truth, I am almost afraid to go alone."

"I shall be very glad, indeed, to go; when shall we start?"

"Let us start Monday, and return Friday, as before," replied Drysdale.

"Very well," said Andrews. "I shall be ready on time."

At the first opportunity, Andrews informed Green of their intended visit, and told him that in order to insure the success of their plan, it would be best for him to ride out to the plantation, also, on Wednesday or Thursday. He could thus be on hand in his ghostly capacity whenever wanted. Green promised to be at a certain spot, near the plantation, on Wednesday afternoon, to receive instructions from Andrews, and all their arrangements were then completed.

Andrews took breakfast with Drysdale before starting, Monday morning, and at table, Mrs. Drysdale said:

"Aleck, Mrs. Potter is so far recovered, that I guess we shall drive out to the plantation on Wednesday or Thursday, and spend a day or two with you."

"That will be delightful," replied Drysdale, "and we shall look for you with great pleasure."

"Well, if the ladies are coming at that time, I hope they will bring our mail, for I expect an important letter," said Andrews.

"Oh, certainly," said Mrs. Drysdale; "and, if anything should prevent us from coming, I will send your letters by a servant."

Andrews had written to me of the intended visit to the plantation, and he was anxious to receive any instructions I might send, before he returned to town.

The two gentlemen mounted their horses and cantered off. Drysdale appeared in better spirits than at any time for several weeks, and by the time they reached the plantation, he was quite gay and cheerful. He had a great deal to attend to, and Andrews gave him very considerable assistance. They were kept quite constantly busy until Wednesday noon, when Mrs. Drysdale and Mrs. Potter arrived in a carriage, bringing the mail. As Andrews had expected, there was a letter for him, in which I instructed him to have Green appear to Drysdale, in the small grove of trees, where he had acted so queerly during their last visit. From Drysdale's manner in this grove, I had concluded that some of the money was buried there, and I therefore, considered it a good place for the ghost to appear.

On reading my letter, Andrews remarked that he should be obliged to go to Atkinson, to send a telegram, as his letter required an immediate answer, but that he should return the same evening. This, of course, was only an excuse to get away to meet Green, and so his horse was brought up at once, and he rode away. Green was punctual at the rendezvous, and Andrews gave him full instructions; he was to remain in sight of the house, on the side near the little grove of trees, until an opportunity should occur to appear before Drysdale. Andrews then took a long ride over the country, so as to delay his return to the plantation until after dark. During the evening, Mrs. Potter told him that Drysdale had visited the little grove that afternoon, but she was, of course, unable to follow him.

The next evening, after supper, Andrews proposed taking a short walk, and they all started out together. By chance, they took the direction of the little grove, previously mentioned, and they were all in fine spirits. Mrs. Potter, however, was obliged to walk very slowly, owing to her injured knee, and Mrs. Drysdale kept her company; the two gentlemen were, therefore, some distance in the advance, when they reached the edge of the grove. Drysdale had been unusually cheerful until then, but as they entered the shadow, he began to lose his gayety, as if something disagreeable had been suggested to him. It was now approaching twilight, and he turned toward Andrews half pettishly, and said:

"Don't go into that dismal place; let us stay out in the open walk. I never like to go into such ⸺"

The words died on his tongue, and he nearly fell down from fright. There, crossing their path in the sombre shades of the grove, was that terrible spectre with its ghastly face, measured step, and clotted hair. It passed into the deep recesses of the grove, while Drysdale watched it like a condemned criminal. As it moved out of sight, he fell to the ground like a dead man, and Andrews called for help. Mrs. Drysdale hurried up in great alarm, and took her husband's head in her lap, while Mrs. Potter chafed his hands and held her vinaigrette to his nostrils. Mr. Andrews quickly called some negroes from the house, and they carried their unconscious master to his room. He was soon restored to his senses, but he was in a pitiable condition. The least sound made him start like a person in the *delirium tremens*, and he muttered to himself constantly. Finally he caught Andrews by the hand and said:

"Andrews, didn't you see that horrible ghost?"

"No, indeed; I saw no ghost," replied Andrews. "Did either of you see it?" he continued, turning to the ladies.

They both answered negatively.

"If there really had been such a thing we certainly should have seen it," said Mrs. Potter.

"Well, I know that I saw it, and it is terrible to think that I should be the only one to whom this thing appears," said Drysdale.

Andrews handed him a drink of brandy, which revived his strength a great deal, and he again began to talk about the ghost.

"I can't understand, Andrews, why you didn't see it," he said; "it passed within fifty feet of us, and it was truly terrible."

"It is certainly very strange," replied Andrews. "Here are three persons who did *not* see it, yet you insist that you did. What did it look like? You have never yet described it to me."

Drysdale made no reply, but a look of renewed dread came over his face, and he reached for more brandy, which was given him.

"It surely must be some disease of the brain," said Mrs. Drysdale, tearfully, "for he frequently imagines that he sees strange sights, and I am afraid to think what will happen. If he would only go to some watering-place, and put himself under the care of a reliable physician, he would soon get better."

"The doctors can do me no good, my dear," he said, controlling himself by a great effort; "do not be alarmed, but let me go to sleep for a while, and I shall be better."

Mr. Andrews and Mrs. Potter left the room in a few minutes, as Mr. Drysdale evidently wished to be left alone. They had ample opportunity for consultation, and they decided that Green had better stay near by all night, to watch the house and the grove.

"If that is to be done," said Mrs. Potter, "I will go and put up a lunch which you can take to him, since if he is to remain out there all night, he will not be able to get anything to eat, and you know that a hungry ghost cannot do as well as one which is well fed."

She soon prepared a large lunch, and added to it a small bottle of wine, which she gave to Andrews. He immediately hastened out to the grove, and found Green at a point where they had agreed to meet. He gave the food to Green, and told him to keep a close watch on the house all night; in case of anything occurring he was to tap on the window of Andrews' room, which was on the ground floor. Andrews then returned to the house, leaving Green to eat his lunch, drink his wine and keep watch.

The night was damp and warm, and the insects were particularly active, so that Green's duty was none of the pleasantest. The hours slipped wearily by until after midnight, when he saw a white figure emerge from the house and approach the little grove. He hastily gained an open spot where, in the bright starlight, he could be plainly seen, and, as Drysdale advanced, he slowly paced toward him. To Green's astonishment, Drysdale passed within two feet of him without noticing his presence in any way; they passed so close to each other that Green was forced to step to one side, yet Drysdale walked slowly on until he reached the grove. Here he walked around a moment or two and then returned to the house. Green immediately tapped at Andrews' window and related what had occurred. There being no new developments, Green returned to the wood where he had picketed his horse, and then rode back to Atkinson.

CHAPTER VIII.

FRIDAY morning Drysdale appeared at breakfast and tried to appear natural and at ease. He spoke of his peculiar hallucination, but his remarks were simply repetitions of those he had frequently made before. Andrews again requested him to describe the appearance of the spectre, but Drysdale seemed averse to continuing the conversation on that subject, and so it was dropped.

Immediately after dinner they started for Atkinson, the gentlemen on horseback, and the ladies in the carriage. As Andrews could offer no plausible excuse for detaining them, Mrs. Potter was obliged to try what she could do. By making two calls on acquaintances living along the road, she was enabled to keep back their arrival much later than Drysdale liked, though not late enough for her purpose. It was too early to have Green appear, as there were so many people traveling on the road that he might be seen by others and the trick exposed.

It was quite evident that Drysdale was in a miserable condition. He was sure that he had seen the ghost of George Gordon, and he was in a state of momentary dread and suspense. He had entertained thoughts of leaving the place, but he dared not. Like Eugene Aram, he pictured himself as continually haunted by the spirit of his victim, and he feared lest others should see it, and accuse him of the murder. His health failed rapidly; his form was emaciated, his cheeks hollow, his eyes haggard and sunken. It was clearly only a question of time how soon he confessed or went insane.

Green continued his night watches about the house, and again one night Drysdale passed out to the creek and acted as before. This time, however, he had his clothes on, and as he passed Green at arms length, it seemed almost incredible that he should have failed to see him. Green took particular pains to identify the exact spot where Drysdale had searched in the water, and he marked it carefully by placing a stone on each side of the bank opposite where Drysdale had stopped.

The following night Mrs. Potter got up and went into Drysdale's room, where he was sleeping alone. She then dropped some blood on his pillow, on the floor, and around the bed. Then passing out, she left the trail as before from the house toward Rocky Creek. Drysdale was horrified early next morning when he saw the bloodstains. He groaned piteously as he walked about the room, and then followed the spots out to the front gate. On seeing that they continued beyond this, he came back with a most dejected and helpless look. Mrs. Potter saw him go into his room, and, by looking through the keyhole of the connecting door, she was enabled to see that he was engaged in washing out the spots on the floor and bed clothes. He did not appear at the breakfast table, but his wife told Mrs. Potter that he had had another severe attack of bleeding during the night, and that he was very weak in consequence.

During the forenoon Mrs. Potter went in to see Mr.

Drysdale, whom she found in great distress physically and mentally. He was anxious to see Mr. Andrews, and his wife sent a message to the hotel at once. In about an hour Andrews came in.

"I am sorry to find you feeling so bad this morning," he said. "You were looking quite well last evening. What is the trouble? Wouldn't you like me to go for a doctor?"

"No, thank you; I shall get along better without physic," replied Drysdale. "I was feeling unusually well last evening, but I had a severe attack of bleeding last night, and I am very weak."

"Is there anything I can do for you?" asked Andrews.

"Well, yes; there are some papers in my office that should be sent to Captain Rowland, a planter in the west end of the county, and as it is important that they should be delivered soon, I should be greatly obliged if you would get them and send them off."

"Certainly, certainly," said Andrews; "where shall I find them?"

"They are in the left-hand pigeon-hole of my upright desk, in the office, and you can send them by Dan. Marston, who lives near the court-house; he is very faithful and trustworthy. Any one can tell you where to find him."

"Oh, I know Dan.," said Andrews, "he has done several errands for me. Where are your keys?"

"They are on the bureau, yonder; but, Andrews, I wish you would come back after you have sent the papers. I always feel better when I hear you talking;

when I am alone I keep thinking about that spirit, and I tell you it is terrible. You will come back, won't you?"

"Oh, certainly; I shall be glad to keep you company while you are under the weather."

When Andrews started off with the keys, a sudden thought flashed into his mind, and he first went to his room, where he obtained some blood, of which he had quite a supply. He then went to Drysdale's private office and dropped some blood on the desk, chairs and floor, and also on the wrapper of Captain Rowland's papers. He was well known to the deputy clerk, and so no one questioned his right to go to Drysdale's desk. On leaving the private office, he locked the door, and hurried back to Drysdale's house with the papers. He entered Drysdale's room in an excited manner, and said:

"Why, Drysdale, you must have been bleeding at the office, for there is blood on your chairs, desk, and on these papers; look there!"

As he spoke, he held out the package with its dull, crimson stain. The shock was too much for Drysdale, and he fainted away instantly. It was sometime before he revived, but finally, he was able to talk again.

"Please take the wrapper off those papers," he said feebly, "and put them into another. They are copies of papers in a law case now in court, and I would not like them to go out in that condition."

Andrews agreed to fix them all neat and clean before sending them, and he then went out to attend to it. On his way down town, he met Mr. McGregor, to whom he related what he had done, and its effect.

"Mr. McGregor," he continued, "I think it would be

a good idea to sprinkle some blood in the bank, on the floor, and on the desk, where young Gordon used to stand; also, to put some blood and hair on the canceling hammer. Do this in the evening, and arrange to have some one enter the bank with you in the morning; then, the story will be circulated until Drysdale will hear it, and it may have a powerful effect upon him. I think Mr. Pinkerton would approve the plan, if he were here."

Mr. McGregor thought favorably of the suggestion, and he agreed to act upon it, as soon as possible. Andrews then went back to Drysdale's office, wiped up the blood spots, and put Captain Rowland's papers into a new wrapper. Having sent them off, he returned and passed the afternoon with Drysdale.

The latter was in a terrible condition; he seemed like a man suffering from hydrophobia, so sensitive were his nerves, and so depressed was his mind. His thoughts could turn in only one direction, and that was toward remorse and fear.

> "'Tis guilt alone,
> Like brain sick frenzy in its feverish mood,
> Fills the light air with visionary terrors
> And shapeless forms of fear."

Through advices from Andrews, I was aware that things were approaching a crisis, and I therefore, went immediately to Atkinson, in order to be ready for any emergency. I arrived there the very morning chosen by Mr. McGregor, to carry out his project of sprinkling blood at the bank. He had arranged, by apparent accident, to have two planters enter the bank with him, and in fact, it happened that four gentlemen were present at ten o'clock when he opened the bank. They all entered together, and when Mr. McGregor had taken down the blinds, he went inside the bank railing. As he did so, he uttered a sudden exclamation, which caused the others to follow.

"What can this mean!" he said, in an excited tone.

The other gentlemen gathered around the ghastly scene and examined the blood, which lay in a pool on the floor, and in spots on the furniture and wall. The canceling hammer, stained with blood, and clotted with hair, lay close by, and every one was reminded of the appearance of the place, the morning after George Gordon's murder.

"What can have happened?" asked old Mr. Gordon, who had just entered. "Surely, no one was murdered here last night."

"Ah! I fear it is done by poor George's spirit!" exclaimed O'Fallon, who was a very superstitious man. "This looks just as it did that fatal morning, except that the body is not here. His spirit must be uneasy at the failure to discover his murderer."

By this time, Flanders and several others, had entered the bank, and the appearance of things there, was soon circulated throughout the town. The excitement about the murder, was revived in all its original importance, and many were the speculations about the mysterious affair.

Drysdale felt rather strong that morning, and about noon, he walked down to his gate. While there, some of his neighbors passed on their way to their homes, and they were all anxious to tell him about the new sensation at the bank. On hearing the news, Drysdale dragged himself into the house and went to bed. There he lay, groaning and sobbing piteously, and when Andrews called in the afternoon, he was so helpless that Andrews insisted on calling a physician. In a short time he returned with Dr. Sprague, who examined the patient, and prescribed for him. Dr. Sprague said that Drysdale would speedily recover with a proper amount of rest and sleep. Wakefulness and nervous irritation seemed to be the trouble with him, and the doctor told Andrews that he had prescribed morphine. He said that there was nothing serious to fear unless fever should set in, and if any symptoms should show themselves it would be necessary to call him immediately.

Upon leaving Drysdale, Andrews came to me to report. I had arranged with Mr. McGregor, to pay a visit to the creek that night, to search the spot which had been visited so often by Drysdale. I therefore sent Andrews back to offer to remain with Drysdale during the night. This arrangement pleased Drysdale very much, and he was quite touched by Andrews kindness. I also instructed Green to watch Drysdale's house, so as to be ready to appear before Drysdale, in case the latter left his house. He was to cross and re-cross Drysdale's path, until Drysdale should take notice of him, while Andrews was to be at hand immediately, pretending that he had fallen asleep during his watch, and on waking up suddenly and finding Drysdale gone, had come out in search of him.

I told Mr. Bannatine and Mr. McGregor, to bring a wheelbarrow, pick-axe, and large shovel with them, since we should probably need the two latter to dig up the gold, while the wheelbarrow would be handy to carry it home. Everything was provided for in advance, and I felt confident of the success of our expedition.

"He was forced to visit the spot where his blood-stained treasure was concealed, even in his hours of repose." —Page 91.

CHAPTER IX.

THE night was clear and bright, and everything was favorable for our work. At twelve o'clock, we met as previously agreed, and hastened to the banks of Rocky Creek, at the spot which Green had pointed out to me that day. On reaching the designated place, I threw off my coat and waded into the creek. I soon found a large flat stone, which I removed to one side. I was just beginning to dig under it, when Green hurried up and told me that Drysdale had left the house, and that he was only a short distance behind. We quickly hid ourselves in the underbrush, and in a few moments Drysdale appeared. Green passed him back and forth, several times, but Drysdale paid no attention to him whatever. Suddenly the thought flashed upon me, that he was walking in his sleep, and I soon saw that such was the case. All of his midnight promenades were now accounted for, and it was not strange that he had not noticed Green. So great was the man's anxiety and nervous dread of discovery, that he could not rest in quiet, and he was forced to visit the spot where his blood-stained treasure was concealed, even in his hours of repose.

He now waded into the creek, as before, but he remained a much longer time than usual, as he was unable to find the large flat stone in its accustomed spot. Finally, he discovered where I had thrown it, and he immediately replaced it in the very hole whence I had taken it. He then returned to the house, and went to bed.

I again removed the stone, and while Mr. McGregor handled the pick-axe, I plied the shovel vigorously. In a very few minutes, we struck a piece of wood which gave back a hollow sound. This encouraged us to renewed activity, and we were richly rewarded by unearthing a large cheese-box, whose weight gave ample proof of the value of its contents. Having replaced the flat stone where we first found it, we put the box on the wheelbarrow, and took turns in wheeling it to the bank, where we soon broke it open and discovered, as we had expected, that it was full of gold coin in rouleaux. The counting of this large sum of money was rather tedious, but it was finally accomplished satisfactorily, and the result showed that only eighty dollars were missing.

The officers of the bank were in high glee, and they asked me whether I had any hope of recovering the paper money.

"If I am not mistaken," I replied, "I shall find the paper money also, within twenty-four hours. I shall go to Drysdale's plantation to-morrow night, and shall search the ground in that group of trees of which you have already heard so much. I think we shall find there all the paper money."

The next day, Drysdale and Andrews remained together constantly; indeed, Drysdale did not seem willing to let Andrews leave his sight for a moment. He was perfectly helpless and inert. In the evening, I met my companions of the night previous, and we drove out to Drysdale's plantation, taking along the necessary tools. We secured our horses in the grove, and then Green led the way toward the spot where Drysdale had examined the ground. On making a close examination with our dark lanterns, we discovered a piece of sod which had evidently been taken up, for the edges had not yet joined with the surrounding turf. We quickly pulled it up and began to dig beneath it; as before, our search was rewarded after a few minutes of labor. At the depth of two feet, we came upon a large candle-box, which we carefully dug up and placed in one of our buggies. There was apparently, nothing more concealed in this spot, and so we replaced the earth, packed it down, and put the piece of sod back into its place. We then returned to Atkinson, where we arrived just before daylight. The bank officers immediately opened the box, and counted the paper money contained therein; it was found to agree exactly, with the sum stolen from the bank. The packages of bills were replaced in the box, which was then locked up in the vault.

I sent instructions by Andrews to Mrs. Potter to again make use of the blood about Drysdale's house, and I also ordered Green to keep watch during the night. The next morning Andrews reported that Drysdale's terror on discovering the blood had been greater than he had ever shown before, and that he was fast breaking down. I therefore held a consultation with the bank officers.

"Now, gentlemen," I said, "we have recovered the money, and we have sufficient evidence to convict the murderer. I think it is time to arrest him; don't you?"

To tell the truth, I was in no easy frame of mind myself. I was morally sure of Drysdale's guilt, but I had no legal evidence which was sufficient to convict him in case he should maintain his innocence. Moreover I had assumed a terrible responsibility in taking such extreme measures with him, for there was danger that he might go insane without confessing his guilt, and in that case my position would have been really dangerous. I should have been accused of driving him crazy with no proper justification for my actions, and the result might have been most disastrous to me. The fact that I, an unknown man from the North, had driven a high-toned Southern gentleman insane, would have been sufficient to hang me by the summary process of lynch law.

The fact that part of the money had been found on his plantation, would be only circumstantial evidence, since another man might have buried it there as well as Drysdale. His visits to the spots where the money was concealed, were not conclusive of guilt, since he was a somnambulist, and in his sleep-walking he was not responsible for his actions. Mrs. Potter suggested to me that he might have been sleep-walking the night of the murder, and (while in that condition,) he might have followed the murderer to the spot where the gold was hidden; it would then be nothing strange that he should go to the same spot in his subsequent night-wanderings.

It will thus be easily understood that during the remainder of my connection with the case, I was in a highly wrought up frame of mind. Indeed, when I came to make the arrest, it would have been hard to tell whether Drysdale or I was the more excited. In reply to my question, Mr. Bannatine instructed me to take whatever course I saw fit, as they were all perfectly satisfied with my management of the affair. I learned from Andrews that Drysdale would visit his office that afternoon, as there were some important matters requiring his attention. Drysdale had told Andrews that he intended to put the office in the charge of a deputy for a time, so as to enable him to go off to New Orleans on a visit of several weeks, and he desired that Andrews should accompany him. He little thought that the toils were closing around him so rapidly, and that he should never start on his projected excursion.

Having decided to arrest him immediately, I went to the office of an old friend of Mr. Bannatine, a lawyer, who drew up the necessary affidavit upon which I proposed to apply for a warrant. I then called upon the sheriff, and asked him to go before a justice of the peace with me, while I swore to an affidavit for a warrant which I wished him to execute.

"What is the warrant for?" asked the sheriff, as he walked along with me.

"It is quite an important case," I replied, "and I have had the affidavits drawn up by Mr. Wood, the lawyer, and you will see the charge in a few minutes."

"All right," said the sheriff; "let us go to Squire Baker's."

Fortunately we found the justice alone, and having stated that I wished to obtain a warrant, I handed him the affidavit which I had had prepared. He carefully adjusted his glasses and began to read the paper, but in a moment or two he gave a sudden start and dropped the document, in utter amazement. He looked at me keenly and said:

"Do you mean to accuse Mr. Drysdale of murdering George Gordon?"

At this the sheriff was equally astonished, and he said:

"Oh! nonsense; it can't be possible. Why, do you know, my dear sir, that he is one of the finest gentlemen, and one of the most honorable men in Atkinson? Surely you are joking."

"No, I am not joking at all," I replied. "I knew, of course, that you would be greatly surprised and shocked, but the proofs are too clear to admit of any doubt. The matter has been carefully examined by Mr. Bannatine, Mr. Gordon, and Mr. McGregor, and it is at their request that I have come to get a warrant. However, I can soon convince you of his guilt."

"Well, well, it is almost incredible," said Squire Baker, "but if Mr. Bannatine and Mr. McGregor are convinced, I presume there must be strong grounds for suspicion, for they are both very careful men. I certainly hope, however, that it may prove to have been a mistake, and that Mr. Drysdale will be able to show his innocence."

I then made oath to the facts, and the warrant was issued. The sheriff asked me when he should make the arrest, and I told him that Drysdale was then at his office, and he must be taken at once. We accordingly, went straight to his office, where we found him with Andrews. As the sheriff entered, Drysdale said:

"How do you do, Mr. Ringwood? Take a chair."

"No, I thank you, Mr. Drysdale," said the sheriff in a sympathetic tone; "the fact is, I am here on a very unpleasant duty, and I cannot stay long. I have a warrant for your arrest, Mr. Drysdale."

"Warrant for me! what for?" exclaimed Drysdale, huskily.

"It is for the murder of George Gordon," replied the sheriff.

"Who charges me? I——"

Drysdale could only shriek the above, ere he fell back into a chair almost lifeless. In a few minutes, he recovered somewhat, and the sheriff said:

"Mr. Pinkerton here, has made an affidavit to the charge, and he seems to be acquainted with the grounds for accusing you; suppose you walk down to the bank with us."

Drysdale gazed at me steadily for a moment, and then said:

"Let me look at the warrant."

He was trembling like an aspen leaf, while he was reading it, and when he had finished, he expressed a willingness to go with us, if Andrews would go too. It was now after banking hours, and the bank was closed, but the officers admitted us. After the door had been closed, I turned to Drysdale and said:

"I have the unpleasant duty, Mr. Drysdale, of charging you with the murder of George Gordon, in this bank; have you any denial to make?"

This was the signal to Green, and as I finished speaking, he passed from behind the desk, where he had been seated, across the spot where Gordon's body had fallen. He was made up exactly like Gordon, as on previous occasions, and though he was in sight only a second, it was enough. Drysdale gave a shriek, and fell lifeless, as the apparent ghost disappeared in the vault. It was done so quickly, that even the sheriff was puzzled to determine what the apparition was. Restoratives were applied, and Drysdale soon revived.

"Great God!" he exclaimed. "Where is George Gordon? I am sure he was here. Did you see him, Andrews?"

No one answered, and seeing that we were all looking at him in amazement, he sprang to his feet, exclaiming:

"I deny the charge you have made against me; it is false in every particular."

"Then, Mr. Drysdale," said I, "you will probably deny that you buried the gold, which was taken from this bank, in the bed of Rocky Creek. Here it is," I added, uncovering the box, which had been placed near by.

He said nothing, but hung his head, and drew a long breath.

"Will you also deny that you buried the paper money in a grove near your house, on your plantation?" I continued, showing him the candle box.

He still said nothing, and I made a motion to Andrews to have Green ready for a re-appearance. Then I went on speaking.

"This money has all been identified as that which was stolen from the bank; it was found as I have stated. I also have here a partly burned note of yours, which you used to light the fire in the grate. I have examined these fragments of buttons, and I find that they are exactly like those on the coat which you brought home from New

"Drysdale gave a shriek, and fell lifeless, as the apparent ghost disappeared in the vault."—Page 98.

Orleans just before the murder; they were found in the grate yonder, where you burned your coat, but there is enough left of them to identify them. But if you are not satisfied with this evidence, that we can prove you are guilty, I will even call upon the murdered man himself, to testify against you."

As I spoke, Green slowly glided out toward us, with his white, set face, and bloody hair. Drysdale covered his face with his hands, dropped into a chair and shrieked:

"Oh! my God! I am guilty! I am guilty!" and he sank back, but did not faint.

Green instantly retired, whence he came, and Drysdale continued speaking, as if he obtained relief by confessing his crime.

"Yes, I am guilty, and I have suffered the tortures of the damned since that frightful night. I do not know what made me do it, but I have never known a moment's peace since then. My mind has been occupied with that money constantly, and even in my sleep I would dream about it. Oh! it is terrible!"

"Have you ever gone to look for it at night, Mr. Drysdale?" I asked, as I wished to know whether he was aware of his somnambulism.

"Oh, no; I would not dare to go near it, but it has haunted me always."

"How did you come to murder George?" I asked.

"I can't tell," he replied, in a choking voice; "it all occurred like a dream."

"What motive did you have? You surely could have

got money without resorting to robbery, much less murder."

"No, I could not. People think I am wealthy, but the fact is I lost a great deal of money in speculating when I went to New Orleans, a few months before the murder, and although I have a good deal of property, I had no ready money, and I could not work my plantation properly for want of it. I had purchased seven slaves from a man in New Orleans, and I could not pay for them. He was pressing me for the money, about twelve hundred dollars, and I came down to the bank to get the money from George. I had only three hundred dollars in bank, and so I gave my note for the remainder. While George was counting out the money, I was taken with a sort of insanity, and I struck him with a large hammer which happened to be at hand. Then I carried off the money and buried it, since which time I have never touched it. It has been a curse to me. This is all I have to say now."

I turned to Mr. Bannatine and said:

"I have now done all that I can do in this matter, I think."

"Yes, you have completed your task, and the law must now take its course," he replied. "Mr. Ringwood, you had better take charge of Mr. Drysdale."

Drysdale rose from his chair, wearily, and said:

"I am glad the end has come at last. This affair has been killing me by inches, and I am glad I have confessed."

The sheriff then touched him on the shoulder and said that he must go.

"Yes, I am ready," he replied, "but please let me speak a few words privately, to Mr. Andrews; I want to send a message to my wife," he added, with a sob.

He and Andrews then stepped into the small private office, and Andrews closed the door behind him.

"Andrews, my friend," said Drysdale, convulsively, "I beg you to break this news to my poor wife. God help her and the children. Tell her that I feel better for having confessed, and whatever happens she must keep up her courage. Now, my dear friend, good bye. Tell the sheriff to come here and take me to jail."

He wrung Andrews' hand warmly as the latter stepped to the door, but before the latter had reached us, we heard the ringing report of a pistol shot. We made a simultaneous rush for the little room, but we were too late. There, quivering on the floor, with a bullet in his brain, lay the murderer of George Gordon. The crime and the avengement had occurred in the same building, only a few feet separating the spot where the two bodies had fallen. The somnambulist had walked on earth for the last time.

THE END.

THE MURDERER

AND THE

FORTUNE TELLER.

THE MURDERER

AND THE

FORTUNE TELLER.

CHAPTER I.

ONE sultry day in the summer of 185-, I arrived in Chicago, from a tour I had been making through the Southern States. I had attended to a portion of the accumulated business which I found awaiting me, when a gentleman entered the outer office and asked one of my clerks whether he could see me immediately on some very important business. Mr. Howard saw by the gentleman's appearance, that the matter must be one of great consequence, and, therefore, ushered the visitor into my private office, without asking any questions.

"Mr. Pinkerton, I believe?" said the gentleman, as he advanced toward me.

"Yes, sir," I replied; "what can I do for you?"

He took a letter from his pocket and handed it to me. I motioned him to be seated, while I read the letter. I found it to be from my old friend Chapman, a lawyer in

New Haven, Connecticut, introducing the bearer, Captain J. N. Sumner. The letter stated that Captain Sumner was a resident of Springfield, Massachusetts, near which place he owned a farm. He had a moderate fortune, and he was a most estimable man. Mr. Chapman had known him for many years, during which time he had always borne himself in an upright, straightforward manner, free from all reproach. Lately, however, he had become involved in some very serious difficulties in the West, and Mr. Chapman had advised him to see me, and obtain my assistance in extricating himself from his troubles. Mr. Chapman concluded by saying, that he was confident, that, if any one could aid the Captain, I was the best person to consult.

I had not seen Mr. Chapman for some years, the last time having been while I was attending to some business in which he was interested. He was especially noted as a criminal lawyer being employed quite as often for the prosecution, as for the defense. We were the best of friends, and had cracked many a joke at each other's expense. He did not mention the nature of the Captain's troubles in his letters, leaving that for the Captain to do himself.

While I was reading the letter, I was aware that the Captain was observing me closely, as if desirous of reading my very thoughts. When I had finished, I said:

"Captain Sumner, I am glad to meet you. Any one bearing a letter from my old friend Chapman, is welcome."

As I spoke, I looked straight at him, and took in his whole appearance.

He was apparently, about fifty years of age, but was very well preserved, not a streak of gray being visible in his dark, curly hair. He was slightly above the middle height, and his frame was proportionally powerful, his limbs being well knit, and muscular. His clear, hazel eyes looked frankly out beneath heavy, straight eyebrows, while his large Roman nose and massive chin, gave his face great firmness and determination. His teeth were white and regular, and his smile was unusually sweet and expressive. His face was much tanned from long exposure to the weather, and his hands were large and hard. He was dressed in a quiet, neat suit of gray cloth, well fitting but easy, and there was nothing loud or in bad taste about him. His only articles of jewelry were a gold watch and chain, and a seal ring with a peculiar, plain stone, worn on the little finger of his left hand. I gazed steadily at him for about two minutes, which is about as long a time as I need to obtain a correct opinion of a man's character. I was very favorably impressed by his appearance, and I prepared to hear his story with more interest than I should have had, if he had been a less honest, reliable looking man.

He opened the conversation, while I was still looking straight into his face.

"Mr. Pinkerton," he said, "I have heard a great deal about you from various sources, and I little thought that I should ever require your services; but, lately, while consulting Mr. Chapman relative to a possible flaw in the title to my farm, I also laid before him some other troubles which he acknowledged were so serious as to require the advice and assistance of some one with a training and experience somewhat different from his. He urged me so strongly to state my case to you, and obtain your aid, that I have finally decided to follow his advice, and here I am."

"When did you arrive?" I inquired.

"About a week ago. I looked around for a time to see if my difficulties had diminished, ——" (and he passed his hand nervously through his hair, drawing a long breath) — "but I found they had increased, if anything. Mr. Pinkerton, when I retired from the sea and settled down on my farm, I thought my cares and vexations were over, and that I could find in the peace and tranquility of country life, a rich reward for the hardships I had endured while earning enough to retire on. My father, also, was a sailor many years, and, after passing the best part of his life at sea, in like manner, he was able to live his last twenty years in peace and content upon his farm; there I was reared, until I was old enough to go to sea. I have followed his example; but, instead of enjoying the peace he did, I find that my serious troubles are only just beginning. If I were at sea, I should have no fears, for there I am perfectly at home. No matter how the wind might blow, or the seas roll, I always brought my ship through in safety. I could read the signs of the weather, and could detect the approach of danger from the elements. I *knew* my enemies were there, and that was half the battle. Here, on land, I find it so different; my worst enemies come to me with the smiles and greetings of friends; they express the tenderest wishes for my welfare, and shower upon me the tokens of their affection; then, having fairly won my confidence, they turn upon me when I least expect it, and stab me cruelly. I am a plain, blunt man—often irritable and unjust, I know—still, I never flinch from danger when I can see it; but, the very nature of my bringing up has rendered me unfit to cope with the wiles and subtleties of my fellow man. You, Mr. Pinkerton, it is said, have the power to see direct to the hearts of men through the shams and artifices by which they seek to hide their true characters, and you are the only man who can assist me. Oh, I wish I were back on the sea, far away from all my troubles. I should care but little if I never returned."

He spoke in a low voice, but the tone was clear until the last, when his words were very pathetic. As he closed, his head dropped forward, and he sat gazing fixedly at his ring in an attitude of mournful retrospection.

"Perhaps you had better wait awhile before telling me your story," I suggested.

"Yes," he replied, looking at his watch, "it is now five o'clock, so I will defer making my statement until to-morrow; though I should prefer to make it now, if I had time. The story is a long one, and I shall have to take a considerable portion of your valuable time in telling it. Will you please to name the hour when I can meet you to-morrow, to give you all the facts in the case?"

I had already become interested in the Captain, and, after thinking for a moment how I could best arrange my other business so as to grant him the necessary time, I told him to come at nine o'clock next morning. He said he would be punctual in keeping the appointment; then stepping forward, he took my hand and said, in a very impressive way, "Mr. Pinkerton, I shall meet you if I am alive. I am not afraid of death; I have met it scores of times, face to face, and have never flinched from it; but now I must take care of myself. If I don't come, just look for me at my boarding house."

I glanced quickly at him, but could see nothing wrong about his mind. His eyes were clear and natural; his whole appearance showed him to be a plain, blunt seaman, little disposed to invent imaginary dangers. Still, there was in his manner, a deep melancholy, which showed me that it was not any natural disease that he dreaded, and which caused me to exclaim:

"Why, Captain, you fear death by violence, do you not?"

"Yes," he replied; "but I cannot enter into details at present. I shall try to save myself and meet you to-morrow morning, but if I do not come, please send my body to Connecticut, to be interred near the rest of my family."

He then said good-day and went out, leaving me to speculate upon his peculiar behavior, and to wonder what were the dangers which surrounded him. I was so much pleased with his frank, manly simplicity that I was determined to give him all the assistance in my power.

CHAPTER II.

AT nine o'clock the next morning, Captain Sumner walked into my private office, and I immediately locked the door to avoid interruption. I noticed that he was apparently much more contented than he had been the evening previous; but I said nothing, preferring to have him tell his story in his own way. He began immediately, without wasting time in preliminaries:

"Mr. Pinkerton, I know that you are always busy, and that time is money to you; hence, I shall be as brief as possible. In order to begin right, I must go slightly into my family history. My father owned a farm near Springfield, Massachusetts, where my mother brought up the family while he was away at sea. He was as fine a seaman as ever trod a deck, and became Captain in one of the regular lines of East India packet companies while I was a mere child. I had one brother who died very young, leaving me the only boy of the family. I had two sisters, however, Lucy and Annie. My father took me to sea with him when I was quite a boy, and he put me through such a thorough course of seamanship and navigation that, by the time he was ready to resign his captaincy and retire to his farm, I was promoted to the position of first mate in the same line. This was in 1836.

About this time my mother died, and my sisters took charge of the domestic affairs of the farm. My older sister, Lucy, now Mrs. W. R. Lucas, was twenty-two years old. She was a girl of great firmness of character, and she has since proved herself the best of wives, being very domestic and fond of home pleasures. Annie, my younger sister, was eighteen years of age, and she was then my special pride and delight; as, indeed, she has been all her life. She was tall and slender, but well proportioned and graceful. Her features were regular and expressive, and her complexion was very delicate; yet it has retained its freshness until now, instead of fading, as is the case with most clear, soft complexions. She was then, and is still, a beautiful woman. She was very vivacious and witty, was fond of society, and cared less for domestic pursuits than to have a gay time in a large company. She was petted and indulged a great deal, being the youngest and a beauty, so that she was not often called upon to practice self-denial. It is probably partly due to this lack of restraint during her early years that she never has had the strength of character and devotion to good principles as Lucy."

Here the Captain sighed heavily, and stopped speaking for a minute or two. I handed him a glass of ice-water, which he drank mechanically. He then continued:

"As I before stated, I became first mate when my father retired. The company was a wealthy one, owning a number of ships, so that the chances for promotion were very good. My most intimate friend was a young man named Henry Thayer. We had long been ship-mates together, and had passed through a school of navigation at the same time. He was a thorough seaman, a careful, considerate officer, and a true friend. He was a general favorite on account of his cheerful disposition, and we soon became like brothers. Whenever we returned from a voyage, I would bring Henry out to the farm to spend a few days, and, about the time of my promotion, I found that he had become warmly attached to Annie. At every opportunity, he would run down to see her, and in every foreign port we entered, he would be sure to buy some rare and curious present for her. His affection was reciprocated by Annie, and one day, after I had made two or three short voyages as first mate, I returned to the farm and found Annie wearing an engagement ring. I laughingly asked her when it was to come off, and she replied, with many blushes, that they were to be married on Henry's return from his next voyage. I knew that Annie was very fond of gentlemen's society, so I advised her to try to overcome her taste for dress and company; since, when she was married, her husband would be away from home a great deal, and then it would not look well for her to receive much attention in his absence. She seemed to acknowledge the force of my remarks, and said that she should do all in her power to make Henry happy.

"On returning to New York, I found that Henry had been just appointed first mate, and that I had pleased the company so well that they wished me to take command of a new ship which they were building. I gladly accepted the command, and as the ship was not ready for sea, I returned to the farm, where I spent two months. I was somewhat annoyed at Annie's conduct occasionally, as she received, and apparently enjoyed, the attention of several stylish young men, more than was befitting a girl who was engaged to be married. I frequently ran down to New York to oversee the rigging of the new ship, so that I did not know much about her acquaintances; but once, on my return, I saw a beautiful amethyst ring on Annie's finger.

"'Where did you get that ring, Annie?' I asked.

"She laughed gaily and said:

"'Oh! it isn't mine; a gentleman loaned it to me to wear a few days.'

"My impression was, however, that it had been given to her, and I feared she was forgetting Henry; so I said:

"'That is a strange way of acting, Annie. You are engaged to Henry, and you ought to know that it is a wrong and an insult to him for you to receive a present from another young man. If Henry knew of this, it would make trouble.'

"She recognized the truth of what I had said, but she was determined not to acknowledge that she had done wrong; so she flew into a passion and said, as sneeringly as possible:

"'Oh! so you are left here to watch me, are you? Well, then, just report to him that I can get a better husband than he is, any day. I am not going to shut myself up, like a nun in a convent, for any man.'

"I told her that I had no desire to act the part of a tale-bearer, but that I spoke only for her good; her conscience must tell her that she was doing wrong. I concluded by asking her to stay more at home, and thus prepare for a more domestic life. I did not see the ring after this, but Annie was very distant in her manner toward me; her actions showed as plainly as if she had spoken, that she considered me in the light of an unreasonable guardian, who wished to deprive her of all enjoyment. Her giddiness and perverseness caused me much trouble, and I greatly feared she would become reckless after my departure. She was my favorite sister, however, and no matter how she might treat me, I could never lose my love for her.

"The first voyage in my new ship, was a very long one, and, on my return, I found that there had been many changes in my absence. Henry and Annie had been married for sometime, and Henry was then away at sea. As my father had died shortly after the marriage, Annie was living alone in New York, where I called upon her. She was pleasantly situated, and seemed to have everything that could be wished. Lucy was also married, and was living in Morristown, New Jersey. The old homestead had been sold at my father's death, the proceeds being divided between my sisters. A few thousand dollars were left to me, which I deposited in bank with my savings.

"On my return from another long voyage, I was delighted to find Henry at home with Annie, and they seemed more devoted to each other than ever. After this, I saw Henry but twice—once in Singapore, and once in Calcutta. He was then as much in love with Annie, as when he first married her, and he said that she made him perfectly happy. The last time I met him, he had just been notified that he should be given the command of a fine ship on his return to New York; consequently he was in high spirits.

"When I next arrived in New York harbor, I made it my first duty to call on Annie. Much to my surprise, I found that she was teaching music in Brooklyn, at a very high salary. Her musical education had been very thorough, so that she was perfectly competent; but I could not see the necessity for her to teach. She had had one child, but it had died in infancy, and she was living in a fashionable boarding house. I called in the evening, intending to ask her to accompany me for a walk, but she was surrounded by a brilliant company, among whom were several gentlemen, and all were paying her great attention. She was very stylishly dressed, and, to my great disgust, she seemed to be coquetting with several of her admirers. When I was announced, she led me into the library, as if anxious that the company in the parlor should not know that a hard-fisted, weather-beaten sailor like me, was her brother. Still, she spoke very kindly, and seemed glad to see me. She excused herself from going to walk with me on the ground that she had an engagement to accompany the rest of the party to the theatre; but she said that if I would call some other evening, she would gladly go. I was somewhat puzzled by her surroundings and manners, and I determined to have a quiet talk with her as soon as possible.

"The next day, I went to Boston on very important business, and, on my return, I found Annie plunged into all the gayety and dissipation of New York fashionable life. She certainly presented a very elegant and stylish appearance; yet, my heart ached as I looked at her. How much joy it would have given me to have found her in a quiet little home waiting anxiously for Henry's return.

"I talked with her for sometime about her affairs, and urged her to lead a more quiet life; but she insisted that

Henry approved of her present way of living; of course, I could say nothing further.

"'Henry is not as unreasonable as you are,' she would say. 'He knew how lonely I would be while he was gone, and, therefore, he told me not to mope and pine, but to get into good society, and try to be cheerful and happy.'

"Still, I had an undefined feeling that Annie was in danger, and I wrote to Lucy about her, asking Lucy to induce her to break away from the gay life she was leading. Soon afterward, I went to sea again, and, during my absence, Henry was given command of one of the finest ships in the line. Two years passed quickly away, but, as I was engaged during that time in making short voyages to the West Indies and back, I frequently saw Annie in New York. She seemed to grow more and more estranged from me, however, and her conduct caused me great anxiety. I had seen some things in her deportment, which, though not absolutely wrong, were, to my mind, far from proper; besides, she showed a carelessness of appearances not at all becoming a married woman.

"My next series of voyages were very long, and I was able to see Annie only once or twice in several years. She was now thirty-two years old, and was unusually and strikingly handsome. About this time, I returned from a long cruise, and found Annie still teaching music in Brooklyn. She dressed as elegantly as ever, and seemed very complacent and contented. I invited her to take a walk with me, and we went out toward one of the small city parks. As she swept along beside me, her features all animation, and her eyes sparkling with health and pleasure, I thought I had never before seen any one so beautiful. I did not wonder that Henry was so proud of her, or that he should indulge her so much. We strolled about in the park for a time, and then seated ourselves in a quiet spot.

"'How long is it since you have heard from Henry?' I asked.

"'Why, don't you know that we had a quarrel several months ago?' she answered, with an effort, her face turning very red.

"'Annie, do you mean that you and Henry have separated?' I asked, very much shocked at such news.

"'Yes; that is what I mean. Henry became so strict and unjust with me that I complained to him of his treatment. One word brought on another, until at last he flew into a violent passion and left me.'

"On hearing Annie relate, in such a cool, off-hand manner, how she had driven away one of the best husbands that ever lived, I was perfectly thunderstruck. I had feared that something of the kind might happen, but now that it had really come to pass, I hardly knew what to do or say.

"'Is it possible, Annie!' I said. 'Where did he go?'

"'I don't know,' she replied; 'he left his ship and went off.'

"'But they know at the office where he went, don't they?' I asked.

"'No; he left his ship at short notice. The company tried to keep him, but he would not stay; and, finally, he went off without telling any one where he was going,' answered Annie, beginning to cry.

THE MURDERER AND FORTUNE TELLER. 119

"It seemed to me that she was crying more to avert my displeasure than because she missed Henry; but she was my favorite sister, and I still loved her. Hence, though I deeply regretted and condemned her actions, I could not find it in my heart to characterize her conduct as it deserved.

"'Annie, are you not entirely to blame for this? Remember how many times I have cautioned you against the course you were pursuing. Tell me what led to your separation,' I asked, finally.

"At first she refused to say anything; but, at length, I drew out that reports had reached Henry's ears that she was in the habit of accepting a great deal of attention from a certain gentleman, and that he accompanied her to the theatre very frequently.

"'But,' she said, 'there was nothing wrong in that.'

"Then, on several occasions, Henry asked her to attend the theatre with him; but it so happened that she had a severe headache each time. This made Henry jealous, and he asked her, tauntingly, why she never had a headache when a certain gentleman called. This sneer led to mutual recriminations and bitter language on both sides, until Henry went away in a towering rage.

"I could see the whole trouble. Henry loved her passionately, and her conduct had driven him away in despair. I determined to search for him everywhere, in the hope of bringing them again together, and effecting a reconciliation.

"The day before I sailed on my next voyage, I saw a beautiful diamond ring on Annie's finger.

"'Annie,' I asked, sorrowfully, 'whose ring is that?'

"'Why, mine, of course,' she replied; 'have you never seen it before?'

"'You must have plenty of money to be able to buy such valuable jewelry as that,' I said. 'I think you show very bad taste to display it at this time, when you know that your folly has driven your husband from you,' I added, angrily.

"She hung her head in silence, as if really ashamed, and I went away feeling almost guilty for having spoken so harshly to her.

"My next voyage was to the East Indies, and I made inquiries about Henry at every port, besides 'speaking' every vessel I met at sea, but no one could tell me anything about him. It became evident that he had not only left the service of the company, but that he had disappeared from all the localities where he was known.

"On my return to New York, I hurried over to see Annie early in the evening. She was dressed for the opera, and was evidently expecting some one. She was quite surprised to see me, but she threw herself into my arms and kissed me very affectionately, as she inquired whether I had heard any news of her dear Henry. When I told her of my poor success, she pretended to feel very sorry, though she did not apparently allow her sorrow to interfere with her enjoyment.

"'Well, Annie,' I said, 'you are dressed to go out somewhere, aren't you? Tell me all about it.'

"'Yes,' she replied, 'I intended going to the opera with Mr. Pattmore, but if you do not wish me to go, I will remain at home. You must stay to meet him; he is one of the most perfect gentlemen I have ever met.

He belongs in Massachusetts, but he now owns a large hotel in Greenville, Ohio. Mrs. Pattmore and I are *such* good friends, and all the children think the world of me. I have been out to visit them in Greenville twice, and they made my stay so pleasant that I always speak of their house as my home. Mr. Pattmore is in town on business, and I received a note from him this morning asking me to go to the opera.'

"Mr. Pattmore came in just then, and we were introduced to each other. He was a well-built man of about forty-five years of age, with very agreeable, easy manners. His hair and mustache were jet black, and his features were rather pleasing. His eyes were large and black, but restless and snaky; I noticed that he never looked straight into my face when speaking to me. He was dressed in the height of the prevailing fashion, and he showed a good deal of jewelry. They both pressed me to accompany them to the opera, but as I was not appropriately dressed, I declined politely, and they went without me.

"I had previously learned at the office of the company, that they had not heard anything of Henry, so I sorrowfully returned aboard my ship, almost decided to give up a sea-faring life. I was then fifty years of age, and I thought of buying a farm, where I could settle down at my ease. I knew that Annie was in a dangerous position for a handsome woman — left alone with no one to advise or restrain her — and I wished to take her with me, so as to remove her from temptation. I therefore, wrote to Lucy, asking her opinion, and requesting her to advise Annie to give up her present mode of life.

"Lucy wrote a long letter in reply: she said that she very much feared there was something wrong between Annie and Pattmore; when Annie was staying at Greenville, Lucy had written twice, asking her to come to Morristown, where Lucy lived; Annie had promised to do so, but she had never come. Pattmore, Lucy said, was a prominent politician in Greenville, and he was looking forward to the nomination for congressman. Mrs. Pattmore was a very good woman, of fine appearance and agreeable manners; she was very domestic in her tastes and she delighted in taking care of her home and children. There were three children living, the eldest son being about twenty-one years old, and the other two being quite young. Mr. Pattmore's hotel was very well kept and popular, and he was supposed to be wealthy.

"Lucy's letter added greatly to the anxiety which I felt about Annie, and I was very desirous of resigning my command immediately, in order to settle down on a farm with her, and thus remove her from the temptations of a gay city. I felt sure that nothing more would be necessary than a retired, quiet life for a few months, to prepare her to give Henry a joyful and affectionate welcome on his return. Circumstances, however, made it impossible for me to give up my ship at that time, and, at the earnest request of the directors of the company (in which I had invested a considerable portion of my savings) I consented to make one or two more cruises. Accordingly, I sailed for the East Indies for the last time, and made a very speedy and prosperous voyage. I continued my inquiries for Henry Thayer, but was unable to obtain any tidings of him. On my return, I called to see

Annie, and found her occupying her old position as music teacher in Brooklyn. She said that Mrs. Pattmore had urged her so strongly to visit them that she had accepted the invitation twice during my absence.

"I had hardly reached New York, before I was hurried away again; my ship was hastily loaded with a cargo for Rio Janeiro, and I again sailed in command. The trip was a speculative venture, which resulted very profitably, and, on my return, I asked to be relieved from further service. I was then fifty-three years of age, and I needed rest. The company treated me very handsomely, and I sold my shares at a high valuation. Having settled my affairs with the company, I hurried off to see Annie; but I was surprised to find that she had moved to Greenville, where she was teaching music to Mr. Pattmore's younger children.

"I had bought a farm near Springfield, Massachusetts, sometime previous, and, learning that there was some slight inaccuracy in the deed, I went to New Haven to consult a lawyer — your friend, Mr. Chapman — relative to the title. While there, I wrote to Annie, asking her to come and live on the farm with me. She immediately replied that she was under an engagement as teacher for six months, and that she could not leave Greenville until the end of that time. She said that Lucy had asked her to pay a visit to Morristown, but that she had been obliged to decline the invitation for the same reason. In conclusion, Annie begged me to visit her in Greenville.

"As soon, therefore, as I had settled my business affairs, I went to Greenville to stay a few days. Annie seemed very glad to see me, and appeared to be in excellent health. I repeated my proposal, that she should come to keep house for me on my farm, and she seemed favorably disposed toward the arrangement, though she asked time to think about it. I told her that at my death, I should leave her all my property, and that, meantime, she should have everything she wished. I also tried to talk to her about Henry, but she refused to say much, and seemed desirous to believe that he was dead.

"I found that she had very little to do as a teacher, the children being too young to study; but she was much attached to Greenville, as, to use her own words, 'there were so many fashionable people there.' She used to go out driving with Mr. and Mrs. Pattmore, and sometimes with Mr. Pattmore alone, often going as far as fifteen or twenty miles into the country. I did not at all like the way she was acting, and I determined to use every effort to induce her to return to Massachusetts with me. This visit, Mr. Pinkerton, took place about two months ago.

"After remaining in Greenville a few days, I went to visit Lucy in Morristown. We had a long talk together about Annie, and finally, Lucy confided to me that she feared that Annie was *enceinte.*

"'Good heavens, Lucy! that is impossible!' I exclaimed. 'Our family has never had such a disgrace cast upon it before; it has always maintained its purity. No, no; it can't be possible.'

"'I am not *sure* of it,' said Lucy; 'but I know there is something wrong with her, and I greatly fear that she is a ruined woman.'

"I hardly knew what to say or do, the mere suspicion was such a terrible blow."

Here the Captain became greatly affected; the perspiration started on his forehead in large beads, and he often made long pauses, as he continued. His emotion would sometimes entirely overcome him, so that he could not speak.

"Well," he went on, "Lucy wrote to Annie, and back came the answer fully confirming the horrid suspicion. Annie freely confessed that she was *enceinte*, and that Pattmore was the father of her unborn child. She said that she and Pattmore dearly loved each other, and that she could not bear the thought of separating from him.

"My first impulse was to curse her and never see her again; but my old love for her could not be set aside, and pity soon took the place of anger. I could see that Pattmore had thrown a spell around her by his fascinating manners, and she was completely under his influence. I determined to save her from exposure and disgrace, if possible, and, therefore, started for Greenville immediately. I had intended to speak to Annie in a severe and indignant tone, but she rushed to meet me with such a glad little cry that my anger melted away, and tears sprang unbidden to my eyes.

"'Oh! Annie! Annie!' I exclaimed, 'what have you done! How has this man acquired such a terrible power over you as to make you forget your marriage vows and live a life of infamy with him? Have you no stings of conscience? Think how our sainted mother would feel if she could see her little Annie in the power of a heartless libertine. Return with me at once, and I will forget everything. In the seclusion of my farm, you need not fear the fiery tongue of scandal, and I will be a father to your child.'

"She stood with downcast eyes while I was speaking, but when I had finished she began a vehement defense of her conduct, in the course of which she repeated all the usual arguments of those who wish to ease their consciences when on the downward path.

"Mr. Pattmore, she said, was a perfect gentleman; he loved her, and she returned his affection; it was true, unhappily, that they were both married, but nature had intended them for each other, and she preferred to obey the laws of nature to those of society; Mrs. Pattmore was a very fine woman, but she could not make her husband happy.

"The doctrine of free-love was fully endorsed by Annie, who had learned it all by heart, and she advanced the most extraordinary theories in justification of her conduct.

"For years, she said, she had held the first place in Pattmore's heart, and he had lavished his money upon her freely; the diamond ring I had seen, the rich dresses she had worn, a valuable necklace, and many other articles of jewelry were among the gifts he had showered upon her; they loved each other as husband and wife, and as soon as Mrs. Pattmore should die, Mr. Pattmore would make Annie his legal wife.

"I saw that she was completely infatuated, but I endeavored to show her how false her reasoning was, and to what wicked conclusions it would lead. I asked if she had forgotten Henry, who was liable to return at any moment; she could not marry until she obtained a divorce. Besides, the fact that they were looking forward to, and wishing for Mrs. Pattmore's death, was almost equivalent to committing murder, since to desire any person's death was morally as bad as to murder that person.

"We had a long conversation, and finally Annie agreed to join me in Springfield in a short time. I therefore returned to the farm and prepared to settle down. I received no reply to several letters which I wrote to Annie, but at last she sent me a short note saying that she had changed her mind, and that she should stay in Greenville. I immediately replied that I would not permit her to remain there any longer, and I then went to consult Mr. Chapman about the matter. He acknowledged that he could do nothing, as Annie was her own mistress; but he advised me to see you, Mr. Pinkerton, and obtain your advice and assistance. As it was a very delicate matter, affecting the honor of my family, I did not like to speak about it to a third party, as I feared that the story might be made known publicly, and Annie's reputation would then be ruined. I therefore told him that I should not consult you if I could possibly avoid doing so.

"While I was inwardly debating what was best to be done, I received a note from Annie, asking me to come to her, as she feared that something serious was about to happen. I went at once to Greenville, and found that she had decided to remove the evidence of her guilt by performing an abortion. I tried hard to dissuade her from a step which might result in her own death, but she was resolute in her determination not to wait for the child's natural birth. She said that if I would stay with her until she recovered, she would return to Springfield with me and never see Pattmore again. She spoke very feelingly about Henry, and she seemed so deeply and truly penitent that I was finally won over to her wishes, and I agreed to stay with her until she had an operation performed. I determined to take her to stay with Lucy, at Morristown, at first, and she accordingly prepared to leave Greenville.

"She had a long private interview with Pattmore before leaving, and when she came out I saw she had been shedding bitter tears. As I stepped to the office desk to pay my bill, I saw Pattmore in the clerk's room back of the office, and he, too, seemed very much dejected. I could hardly keep my hands off his throat when I recollected his villainy; but I curbed my temper by a great effort, as I knew that a personal encounter between us would only publish my sister's shame to the world. On our arrival in Morristown, Lucy and I had a long talk with Annie, which was far from satisfactory to me, as I saw that she was still infatuated with Pattmore.

"I thought best to go some distance away from the places where we were known during Annie's trial, and I therefore brought her to Chicago. Here I obtained board in a very respectable family, where there were only a few other boarders. Annie did not show her condition in her appearance at all, and no one could possibly have suspected her. I found a physician named Enfield, who was a noted operator in such cases, and Annie at once placed herself under his treatment.

"I knew that I was about to assist in committing a

great crime, yet I felt that I must shield Annie at all hazards, and so I yielded to her wishes in the matter. Enfield was an expert in such matters, and, in a short time, he brought Annie through in safety. She was recovering fast, when one day, on entering her room, I found Pattmore there. I went out instantly, as I was afraid to trust myself in the same room with him; but, when he had gone away, I besought Annie never again to admit him to her presence. She would make no promises, and finally, she fell back in a swoon. On recovering, she said that she would die if she could not see Pattmore, and I was obliged to drop the subject until she should become stronger. Pattmore remained in town two days, and she insisted on having him with her a great deal of the time.

"I fear that you will consider me very weak and foolish for permitting this; but I have never been able to refuse Annie anything. I knew, moreover, that, in such a case, harsh measures would only add fuel to the flame, and so I continued to humor her, trusting, that in time, she would gradually recover her normal condition, and see the folly of her conduct.

"Pattmore told her, during his visit, that he was in great hopes of receiving the democratic nomination to Congress; and, as the democratic party had a large majority in that district, the nomination would be equivalent to an election. He also said that his wife was in failing health, and that she seemed to grow weaker every day. I could see by Annie's manner, when she told me this, that she hoped to be Pattmore's partner in enjoying the gay life of the National Capital, though she did not say so directly.

"One day, she brought up the subject of wills, and said that she thought every one owning property, ought to make a will. She said that otherwise a man's property, in case of sudden death, might be eaten up by the lawyers and court officials. I admitted the justness of her remarks, and told her that I should follow her suggestion. I was obliged to go East on business for a few days at this time, and, on the way, I left a letter and package with Pattmore, which Annie had asked me to deliver. While in New Haven, I employed Mr. Chapman to draw up my will. Lucy had asked me to leave all my property to Annie, as she had enough for herself and children, while Annie had no one to look to for an honest support, except myself; accordingly, I made my will in that way.

"On my return to Chicago, I hurried to our boarding house to see Annie, and, to my intense disgust, I found Pattmore with her. The sight of him fondling my poor sister, was too much for me: and, although I succeeded in restraining myself from doing him any personal violence, I used the most severe language possible in characterizing his villainy, and in expressing my contempt for him. I concluded, by telling him that the affair must end then and there; that he must never address my sister again, or attempt to see her; and that if he dared to disregard my demand, he must take the consequences. They both hung their heads guiltily, while I was speaking, and when I closed, Pattmore quitted the room without a word. I found that he left town the same day.

"I also went out of the house immediately, being too

excited to talk calmly to Annie; but I returned after supper, and reasoned with her as gently as possible on the impropriety and wickedness of her conduct. She seemed to feel very sorry, and was so penitent that my hopes of saving her, rose considerably. She promised, with tears in her eyes, to overcome her unholy love for Pattmore, and never to see him again. I noticed, however, that when I spoke of my efforts to obtain tidings of Henry, she was very indifferent; but she promised to return to Springfield with me as soon as she was able to travel, and matters began to look more cheerful for the future.

"A day or two after, she received a letter from Pattmore, saying that his wife was seriously ill, and that the physicians considered her life in danger.

"'What is the matter with her?' I asked.

"'I don't know,' she replied; 'Mr. Pattmore does not state what is her disease.'

"I then spoke very harshly about Pattmore, and said that he, above all other men, was hateful to me, because he had ruined her. She replied in his defense, and, as our conversation seemed likely to become bitter, I walked out to allow time for both our tempers to cool off. On my return, I found that Annie had gone out for the first time, since her illness, but she soon came in, saying that she had taken a short walk for exercise. She had regained her good humor, and seemed more like herself than she had for sometime. She again brought up the subject of wills, and I told her that I had made my will while I was in New Haven. She asked me about it, and I told her that I had made her my sole legatee, and that she would be in comfortable circumstances when I died. She seemed very much pleased at this, and said I was a dear good brother; but she hoped it might be a long time before she should become heiress to my property.

"'Who knows?' she said, laughing; 'perhaps I may die first.'

"'That is possible,' I said, 'but not probable. In the course of nature, I ought to die many years before you; and sailors are proverbially short-lived.'

"'Oh, nonsense!' she replied, 'you are so salted and tanned that you will last fifty years yet.'

"She then skipped gaily into the next room and brought out a bottle of ale, to reward me, as she said, for being good. She poured out a glass for each of us, and we drank to each other's good health. In about half an hour I became very sick; I vomited and retched terribly, while my bowels seemed to be on fire. The weather was very warm, and I attributed my illness to some fruit I had eaten, which the ale had disagreed with. I suffered agony all night, but toward morning I became quieter and the pain gradually left me.

"At daylight I casually glanced at my ring, and I was surprised to see that the stone had turned to a creamy white—a sure sign that my life was in danger. You will call me foolish and superstitious, I know, but I cannot help it. A belief in the virtues of this ring is a part of my very nature, and it has always been an unerring guide to me. This ring invariably predicts my good or bad fortune." And so speaking, the Captain held the ring out for me to see it.

I looked him straight in the face, expecting to see some

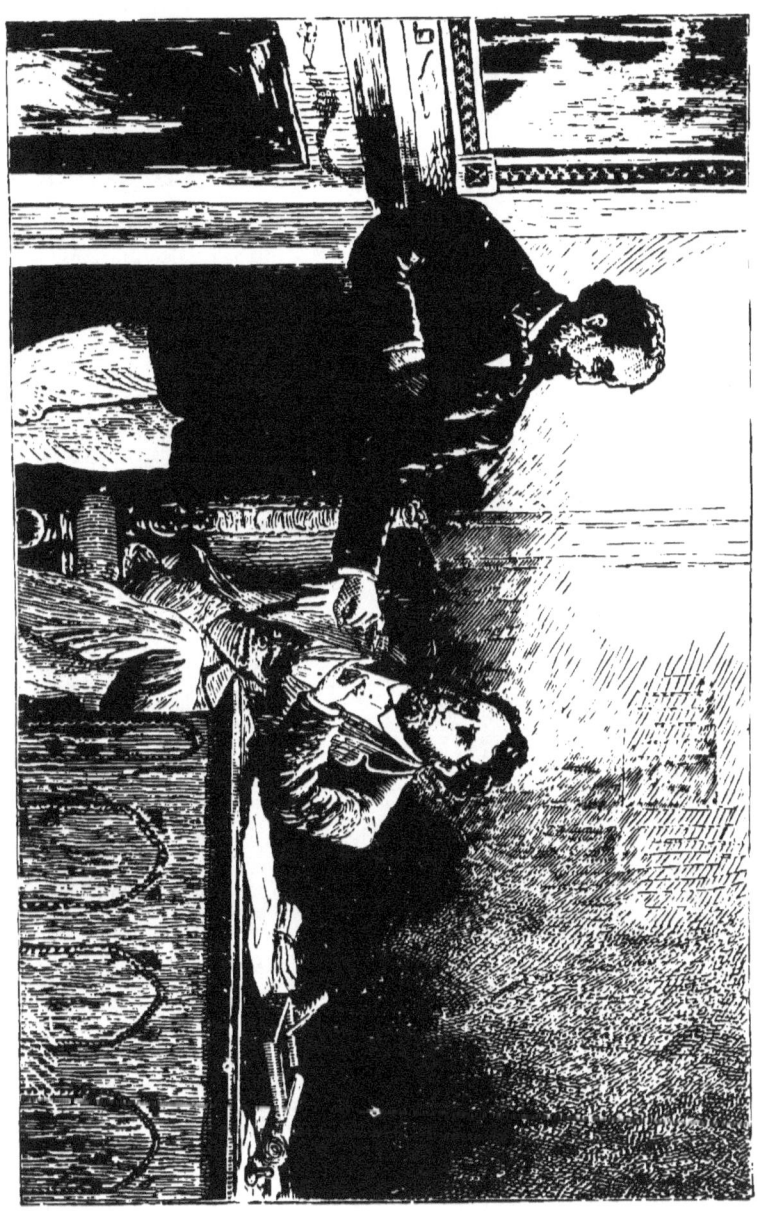

"And so speaking, the Captain held the ring out for me to see it."—Page 132.

signs of insanity, or at least monomania, in his eyes, but there were none. He was evidently perfectly rational, and this belief was apparently as natural to him as a belief in a hereafter, or in any other religious doctrine, is to other people. After a short pause, as I glanced at the ring, he continued:

"Now, you can see nothing strange in that stone, Mr. Pinkerton, but I can. From its appearance I can obtain warning of approaching good or bad fortune. Away out at sea, when a storm is coming, the stone turns black; when enemies are near me it turns the color of blood; and when I am in danger of death, it becomes a creamy white.

"My father once saved the life of a Sepoy soldier, and, as a mark of gratitude, the latter presented my father with three rings of wonderful powers. The Sepoy said that he had obtained them from a Hindoo hermit, far out in the jungle. I have long tried to find other rings possessing the same qualities, but have never succeeded. One of these rings was buried with my mother, one with my father, and I have the third."

I looked at the ring carefully, but could see nothing remarkable about it. The stone was an opal, set in a heavy gold band, peculiarly chased; but, aside from the popular superstition with regard to opals, there was nothing which would lead me to suppose that it possessed any exceptional powers.

"When I saw you last," continued the Captain, "I meant to have asked you to have this ring buried with me, in case I died; but I was afraid you would consider the request too foolish. I wished it buried with me because I did not wish Annie to have it."

"But why do you think Annie would take it?" I asked.

"Because I know she wants it," replied Captain Sumner. "She thinks that it would enable her to make Pattmore love her always, and so she wishes to own it. Now, I think Pattmore is a villain, and I wish to separate her from him and destroy his influence over her. Therefore I do not wish her to get the ring, since its possession will induce her to continue her connection with that man."

I confess that I did not know what to make of the Captain. If he was insane, he certainly had the most impenetrable mask over his insanity that I had ever seen. His eyes were so bright, clear and honest, that the most experienced physiognomist in the world would have failed to observe the slightest trace of cunning, or want of a balanced mind in their expression. During the progress of his story he had continually held his ring where he could see it, and several times had raised it to the light, in a contemplative sort of way, as if he drew some satisfaction from its appearance. He bowed his head in his hands as he ceased speaking, and some moments elapsed before he looked up, though when he did so he was perfectly calm.

"Captain, did you find the ring of any practical value at sea?" I asked.

"Yes; often it has apprised me of a coming storm in time to prepare for it. I have thus passed in safety through many sudden gales of the approach of which I have been warned only just in time to save my ship.

My men always had perfect confidence in my ability to weather the heaviest gale."

"Well, Captain, if you should give that ring to me, would it be equally prophetic in my hands?" I asked.

"But I will not give it to you nor any one else; nor will I part with it, even in death if I can help it," replied the Captain. "The Sepoy told my father, that he must never allow the rings to go out of his family, as they would then lose their powers. I know that the fancy seems strange to you, and, no doubt, you think I am not exactly sane; but I have proved the power of the ring so often, that I know its virtues, and believe in them. I may be able to satisfy you of its value by a practical demonstration yet."

I saw that he was not insane, but terribly superstitious, so I made no further remarks about the ring. He drew his chair closer toward me, and said in a low, painful whisper:

"Mr. Pinkerton, I have positive knowledge that *Annie has attempted to poison me three times.* She put poison in that ale; she afterwards gave me some in a cup of coffee; and, the third ·time, it was administered so secretly, that I do not know when I took it. The first time, I recovered because the dose was too large, and I vomited up the poison so soon that it had not time to act. The second time, I took only a sip of the coffee, and found that it tasted bitter, so I threw it away, though the little I had taken distressed me exceedingly. The third time, I nearly died, and it was only by the prompt attendance of a physician that I was saved. He said it was a metal poison which probably came off from a copper kettle in which some fruit had been cooked. Neither he, nor any one else, ever suspected that I had been poisoned intentionally. When I recovered, I accused Annie of trying to poison me; she denied it vehemently at first, but I said to her:

"'Annie, the ring tells me that I have an enemy near me, and you must be that enemy.'

"I spoke as if positive of her guilt, and, as she is a firm believer in the ring, she finally burst into tears and confessed having given me poison at three different times. On her knees, she begged my forgiveness, and thanked God that my life had been spared. She was so broken down by the thought of her unnatural and wicked purpose, that I feared that she would have a relapse into sickness. She seemed so wholly contrite, that I thought she would never undertake such a terrible crime again, and I freely forgave her."

I looked at the Captain in perfect amazement, hardly able to credit my own senses.

"Can it be possible," I asked, "that your sister admitted that she had tried to poison you?"

"Yes," replied the Captain; "and she said that Pattmore had encouraged her to put me out of the way. He had told her that he would marry her when his wife, (who was now dying) was dead; that I was bitterly opposed to him, and would never consent to their marriage; that if she would poison me, they would be married and go to California to live; and, therefore, that it would be well for her to poison me before Mrs. Pattmore died."

"What!" I exclaimed, "is Mrs. Pattmore dying? What is her disease?"

"I do not know," replied the Captain; "but I fear that *she, also, has been poisoned.*"

"How long is it since you had this talk with Annie?" I inquired.

"About three days ago, and she has been sick abed with excitement and remorse ever since. She says that she expects to hear of Mrs. Pattmore's death at any time, and she is sure that Pattmore has poisoned her. Mr. Chapman told me, when I last saw him, Mr. Pinkerton, that you were the only person who could help me; and so I have come to you to save Mrs. Pattmore and my sister. I feel that Mr. Chapman was right, Mr. Pinkerton, and I beg you to give me your assistance — I will pay you liberally."

CHAPTER III.

WHEN the Captain had finished his almost incredible story, I hardly knew what to make of it. It was impossible to doubt his word; yet it seemed almost equally hard to believe that his sister could have tried to murder him. Pattmore's intention of killing his wife in order to marry Annie, was another piece of cold-blooded villainy which was almost past belief. The question frequently came into my mind: Are all the parties in their right minds? After I had thought about the matter in silence a few minutes, I said:

"Well, Captain Sumner, yours is certainly a strange case, and I cannot give you any answer until I have had time for reflection. Return in three hours and I will then tell you my decision. I will help you if I possibly can do so."

He rose to go, but stopped a moment as he reached the door, and said, with the utmost simplicity and confidence:

"I *know* you can help me if you will do so, and no one else can."

After he had gone, I sent a man to the Captain's boarding house with instructions to learn all he could about the boarders. He reported that, among others, there was a Captain Sumner boarding there with his sister, Mrs. Annie Thayer. My detective also learned many things about the Captain and his sister which corroborated the account given by the Captain. Having satisfied myself that the Captain's story was true—in part at least—I sat down to reflect upon the strange medley which he had told me.

Mrs. Thayer had, undoubtedly, committed a serious crime against her husband, besides making the attempt on her brother's life; but I could not have her punished, for her brother's object was to save her from the ruin in which her downward course would probably end. Pattmore, however, was a dangerous man, and it would be necessary to proceed with caution in handling him. He seemed to be a villain at heart, and it was probable that he only sought Mrs. Thayer's society in order to gratify his sensual passions. Perhaps the Captain's suspicion, that Mrs. Pattmore's illness was caused by poison administered by her husband, was correct; if so, it would be necessary to act at once, before she should become his victim. It was barely possible that he might intend to get a divorce from his wife and then marry Annie; but I did not consider this supposition a very probable one. He wished to be elected to Congress, and he would not dare to give such an opportunity for scandal as would ensue if he attempted that course. No; poison had been his reliance in one case, and he would not scruple to make use of it again. Mrs. Thayer was probably well informed as to all his plans, but, evidently, she would not willingly divulge anything prejudicial to her lover. Her brother was clearly unable to compel her to confess anything, or he would not have applied to me. Moreover he could refuse her nothing, and he would certainly object to any attempt to force her to give evidence against her will. He admitted that she was weak, vain and thoughtless; that she had been false to her husband; and that Pattmore had completely bewitched her; yet the Captain resolutely stood between her and harm.

She could tell all of Pattmore's secrets if she were so disposed, and it would be easier to get information out of her than out of him; the question was—how shall I go about it?

I reflected that she was very superstitious, as shown by her belief in the Captain's ring; it occurred to me that I might take advantage of that trait of her character to draw her secrets out. Why could I not introduce a fortune-teller to her, and thus learn all I wished to know? The idea seemed to me to be admirably adapted to the necessities of the case. I sketched out, in my mind, a skeleton plan of operations about as follows:

I should entrust the case to one of my female detectives; she would be posted upon all the points of Mrs. Thayer's history; she would be required to learn enough of astrology, clairvoyance and mesmerism, to pass for one of the genuine tribe; the plan would be so arranged that Mrs. Thayer would voluntarily consult this fortune-teller, who would soon gain a complete ascendency over her superstitious nature by revealing to her all her past life; finally Mrs. Thayer could be brought to tell all she knew of Pattmore as a means of aiding the sibyl to read her future.

This plan seemed to me the most feasible of any, and I therefore decided to adopt it in working up the case against Pattmore. After all, he would be the one against whom my efforts would be directed, Mrs. Thayer being only an unconscious instrument in bringing him to justice. In case it could be shown that he had actually attempted to murder his wife, I was determined that he should not escape the swift vengeance of the law.

Just as I had concluded my deliberations, the Captain hurried into my office, the perspiration standing in great beads on his forehead.

"Mr. Pinkerton, I fear we are too late!" he exclaimed in a husky voice. "Annie has just received a telegram from Mr. Pattmore, saying that his wife is dead."

"*Dead!*" I repeated. "Is it possible! When did she die?"

"To-day," he replied.

"It will be an easy matter to discover the cause of her death," I said, after a moment's pause. "We must have a *post mortem* examination held."

"That may be possible," replied the Captain; "but you must recollect that Pattmore has a great many friends in Greenville; that, in fact, he is a prominent candidate for the Democratic Congressional nomination; and, even if he were supposed to be guilty, the party would make a strong fight to protect him, as they could not afford to have him exposed."

"Is it possible that he has so much influence as that?" I asked.

"Oh, yes," said the Captain; "he is a brilliant speaker, and a very agreeable man socially, so that he makes many friends. He is such a wily scoundrel that I fear we shall have great difficulty in tracing any crime directly to him. I do not care whether he is convicted or not, provided I can rescue Annie from his clutches. He has apparently cast a spell over her, and she is wholly controlled by him."

"If that is the fact, we must use strategy, and undermine his plot with a deeper one. I will accept a retainer from you, Captain, and then we will proceed to work up the case."

The financial part of the arrangement having been adjusted, I gave the Captain some advice as to what he should do. I told him that he must place implicit confidence in me, and not try to interfere in any manner with my plans. If he could not do this, I should withdraw at once. He must come in to see me often and keep me well informed; but he must not expect me to tell him about my plans, any further than I should see fit. I should try to show Pattmore's villainous character to Annie, and if I could gather sufficient evidence that he had poisoned his wife, I should bring him to justice. I then told the Captain that he ought to have a quarrel with Annie, at the end of which he should burn his will in her presence, and leave her; on going out, he should tell her that he intended immediately to deposit his ready money in bank, and make a will wholly in favor of Lucy. This would prevent Annie from again attempting his life, as she would have nothing to gain by his death.

The Captain was satisfied to accept my conditions, and he said that he had full confidence in my ability. All that he desired was to save Annie from the power of Pattmore, and from the ruin which would inevitably result from their further intercourse. He then went home to have his quarrel with his sister.

I determined to send a detective named Miller, to

Greenville, to obtain board at the Pattmore House, and, if possible, to become intimate with the proprietor. This part of my plan would require prompt action, as Pattmore might succeed in removing all evidences of his guilt. I therefore, sent for Mr. Miller, and went over all the facts of the case with him, giving him full instructions as to his duties. He was to hail from Bangor, Maine, and to represent that he wished to start in the lumber business in Greenville, if the prospects were good. I told him to post himself thoroughly upon the qualities and prices of all kinds of lumber, lath, shingles, etc., and to read up the local history of Bangor. To make matters easier for him, I gave him a letter of introduction to a lumber dealer in Greenville, with whom I was well acquainted. The next day, Miller was ready, and he took passage to Buffalo by steamer, going thence to Greenville by rail. He then took a room at the Pattmore House, and soon became acquainted with the proprietor.

The same day that I gave Miller his instructions, I sent for Miss Seaton, one of the detectives in the female department, and ordered her to make arrangements to take board in the same house with Captain Sumner and Mrs. Thayer. Miss Seaton was a brunette, about twenty-seven years of age; she was of agreeable appearance and pleasing manners; she had been a school teacher, and was a good judge of human nature. Mrs. Warne, the superintendent of the female department, said that Miss Seaton was very sharp, and that nothing could escape her piercing black eye. She was to cultivate Mrs. Thayer's acquaintance, and endeavor to win her confidence. This would probably be a difficult task; but I told Miss Seaton to be patient and discreet, and not to be discouraged, if she should not be immediately successful. By pretending to be in poor health, she could obtain Mrs. Thayer's sympathy, and their progress toward intimacy would be accelerated. Miss Seaton immediately moved to the City Hotel, whence she set out to look for a boarding place. By a curious coincidence, she could not satisfy herself until she came to the house where Mrs. Thayer was boarding on the North side. There she found a pleasant room adjoining Mrs. Thayer's, and it suited her exactly. That evening at supper, she was introduced to her fellow boarders, of whom there were only three besides the Captain and his sister.

The employment of female detectives has been the subject of some adverse criticism by persons who think that women should not engage in such a dangerous calling. It has been claimed that the work is unwomanly; that it is only performed by abandoned women; and that no respectable woman who becomes a detective can remain virtuous. To these theories, which I regret to say are quite prevalent, I enter a positive denial. My experience of twenty years with lady operatives is worth something, and I have no hesitation in saying that the profession of a detective, for a lady possessing the requisite characteristics, is as useful and honorable employment as can be found in any walk of life.

Previous to the early part of 1855, I had never regularly employed any female detectives; nor were women engaged in that capacity in any part of the Union. My first experience with them was due to Mrs. Kate Warne, an intelligent, brilliant, and accomplished lady. She offered her services to me in the early spring of that year, and, in spite of the novelty of her proposition, I determined to give her a trial. She soon showed such tact, readiness of resource, ability to read character, intuitive perception of motives, and rare discretion, that I created a female department in the agency, and made Mrs. Warne the superintendent thereof.

The work of my female detectives is generally light. Zeal and discretion are the principal requisites, though conscientious devotion to duty, and rigid obedience to orders, are also essential. They are expected to win the confidence of those from whom information is desired, and to lose no opportunity of encouraging them to talk about themselves.

With regard to the moral influence of their duties, I say boldly that it is in no respect different from that of any other position where women are thrown upon their own resources. It is an unfortunate fact in our social system, that no single woman or widow, dependent upon herself for support, can escape a loss of caste and position by working in the great field of business where she comes in competition and contact with men; but, aside from this general prejudice, there is nothing in the detective's duties to make her profession less respectable and honorable than there is in the duties of a lady cashier, book-keeper, copyist, or clerk. The detective's temptations are no greater than those of any of the foregoing who mingle with men in their daily business; while, on the other hand, the safeguards of their virtue are much more numerous, since all the detectives of my agency know that their conduct is under constant surveillance.

There are instances of frequent occurrence where great criminals are successful in hiding all traces of their guilt so effectually as to make their conviction impossible without the aid of the female detective. Most of these men have wives or mistresses in whom they confide to a great extent. The testimony of these women, then, become the sole means by which to convict the criminals, and their testimony can be obtained in only one way—a female detective makes their acquaintance, wins their confidence, and draws out the story of the crime. Such an instance is given in "The Expressman and the Detective," hitherto published.

I have in my employ several ladies of unquestionable purity of life, who are also among the most successful operators on my whole force. I take pleasure in offering this tribute to their ability, and their spotless characters.

The next day the Captain called to see me, and said that, according to my advice, he had quarreled with Annie about Pattmore, and had worked himself into a great rage. Finally, he had torn up and burned his will, saying that he should immediately make another, leaving everything to Lucy.

"So far, so good," said I; "she now will have no motive for poisoning you, so you can rest in peace."

The Captain stated further that he had deposited in bank a few hundred dollars which he had brought with him, so that he felt comparatively safe for the present.

That evening Miss Seaton reported that Mrs. Thayer had left the house shortly after the Captain. Miss Seaton had followed her to the post-office, where Mrs. Thayer had deposited a letter, and had received another at the ladies' window. She had immediately torn it open, read it hastily, and crumpled it in her hand, while slowly walking home. I was very anxious to know to whom she had written, and also who had written to her. I immediately wrote to Miller to watch Pattmore's mail, and to learn whether there were any letters in it from Chicago. If so, I wished him to obtain a view of the handwriting, and, if possible, to get possession of the letters themselves long enough to take copies of them.

The next morning Captain Sumner came in again, but he had nothing to report.

"Does Annie write much?" I asked.

"No, very little," he replied.

"Does she correspond with Lucy?"

"Sometimes, but not regularly."

"Did she not write a letter two days ago?" I inquired.

"No," answered the Captain; "but why do you ask?"

"Oh! for no particular reason; however I wish you would write to Lucy and inquire whether she has received a letter from Annie lately; also whether she has written to Annie."

"Certainly, I will do so now," said the Captain, and, he straightway sat down to write to Lucy.

In a few days, the Captain received a letter from Lucy stating that no letters had passed between her and Annie for over a month. This made it certain that Lucy was not Annie's correspondent.

Miller sent in a report about the same time, saying that he had become slightly acquainted with Pattmore, who was deeply mourning the death of his wife. Even the mere mention of her name was sufficient to draw tears to his eyes, and her loss had so severely affected him that his friends were afraid he would never be the same man that he had been during her life.

Miller had expressed an intention of opening an office in Greenville, and Pattmore had given him some valuable advice and information relative to the lumber market in the interior. Since getting my letter, Miller had noticed that Pattmore had received four letters from Chicago. Miller said that he had not been able to obtain possession of these letters, but he should make a great effort to capture those which might come in the future. He had taken pains to cultivate the friendship of the clerk of the hotel, and he was on such good terms with him as to find it convenient to pass a great deal of time in the office. He had noticed that when the clerk received the mail, all of Pattmore's letters were put into a particular box behind the desk, and he hoped to be able to secure some of them.

I had devoted a large amount of thought to this singular case, and I finally decided that I would go to Greenville in person. I determined to see the coroner and find out what kind of a man he was. If possible, I should induce him to have Mrs. Pattmore's body exhumed and an inquest held upon it.

I had previously written to Mr. Chapman to obtain further information about the Captain and his family, and had mentioned his superstitious belief in the ring. I said that I was not afraid of losing money, as the Captain offered me more than my usual scale of prices; but the Captain's story and his great superstition led me to think that he was a "wee bit daft," and that there was insanity in the family.

Mr. Chapman replied that he had known the Captain's father and mother intimately, but there had been no sign of insanity in any of their actions. They had been, however, firm believers in their rings, and had had the rings which they had worn buried with them. They had been clear-headed, religious people, and it was surprising that they should have had such a superstitious faith in the power of those opal rings. The Captain had always been an honorable, straight-forward man, but he and his sister were even more superstitious than any of the others.

"Well," I thought, on reading Mr. Chapman's letter, "the whole family are a strange medley; but I think I can turn their superstitious credulity to good account, in my efforts to learn whether Pattmore poisoned his wife."

CHAPTER IV.

AS soon as possible, I started for Greenville, to see the coroner; on my arrival, I was so fortunate as to meet Mr. Wells, an old friend, who had formerly been sheriff of the county. He offered to introduce me to his successor, Mr. Tomlinson, who had once been his deputy. Mr. Wells was quite wealthy, and had retired from business. Mr. Tomlinson was an honest, hard working carpenter, who was thoroughly reliable and zealous. Neither of these gentlemen, however, had the shrewdness nor the experience necessary to detect criminals of the character and ability of Pattmore. They were perfectly competent to attend to the small thieves and swindlers of the district, but they were wholly ignorant and unsuspicious of the means by which daring and skillful villains carry out their plans and hide the evidences of their crimes.

They knew Mr. Pattmore well, as he had resided in Greenville for seven years. They stated that he was a scheming politician who could not be depended upon, and that he was trying to get the Democratic Nomination for congressman. Probably, he would not succeed, but he was spending money freely, and he would, therefore, be apt to get some good office. He was not wealthy, but he kept his hotel well, and did a large business. Mr. Wells thought that he used all his money as fast as he made it, either in trying to get votes, or in some other way outside of his business. His wife had been generally esteemed by a large circle of acquaintances.

I told Mr. Tomlinson that I should like to see the coroner, and have him investigate the causes of Mrs. Pattmore's death.

"Oh! that will be easy," he replied, "as I know Van Valkenburgh, the coroner, very well, and we are on good terms. He is a warm friend of Pattmore,— in fact, they are boon companions. He spends most of his time in idling about the Pattmore House, and only yesterday, they went driving together."

"I am sorry to hear that," said I; "for he will not wish to do anything to injure his friend. How can I get an inquest called?"

"I don't know," said Mr. Tomlinson.

"Suppose that I should make an affidavit under an assumed name and hand it to you, could you not serve it on the coroner as a complaint which required his attention?" I asked.

"No; that would not do, as it would involve me in difficulty," replied the sheriff; "but if I should hear people talking about the death of Mrs. Pattmore, and hinting at foul play, it would be my duty to lay the matter before the coroner. Then he, as a friend of Pattmore, could not do otherwise than order an inquest."

I determined to act on this suggestion, and I therefore telegraphed to Mr. Bangs, my General Superintendent, directing him to send two of my detectives, Mr. Green and Mr. Knox, to meet me at the Clarendon House in Greenville. They left Chicago by the next train, and when they arrived in Greenville, I instructed them to go into the office of the hotel and begin a conversation about Mrs. Pattmore's death; having told them what I wished them to say, I sent them in. I had previously arranged that Mr. Tomlinson should be present. Accordingly, they took seats in the main hall in front of the clerk's desk, near which there was a large group of guests and citizens, and began to talk in loud tones.

"Well," said Knox, "there are more cases of death by poisoning than you would suppose. Now, there was a case in this town, only a short time ago, in which I think that poison was used."

"Oh! you mean Mrs. Pattmore," said Green. "Yes, that was a very suspicious affair. Was anything done about it?"

"No," replied Knox; "but every one, who knows anything about the circumstances of her death, believes that she was poisoned."

My men were soon surrounded by an excited crowd, all of whom were anxious to know the grounds upon which their suspicions were based. They replied in vague terms and insinuations, as if they knew a great deal more than they would tell. The news that Mr. Pattmore was suspected of having poisoned his wife, was soon buzzed all through the Clarendon House; and, as soon as the excitement had become general, my men slipped away and joined me in my room.

Sheriff Tomlinson was immediately appealed to by many citizens to require the coroner to investigate the matter, and he finally went to the coroner's office, accompanied by quite a crowd. When the coroner was informed of the reports in circulation, he became quite indignant. "What! *Pattmore poison his wife!*" he exclaimed. "Why, he fairly doted on her, and, since her death, he can hardly assuage his grief. He is a gentleman in every sense of the word, and his character ought to be a sufficient protection against so gross a slander. This is a contemptible invention of his political opponents. I will soon vindicate him, however. I shall have Mrs. Pattmore's body exhumed, and shall call an inquest. Then, if any one has any charges to make, there will be an opportunity for them to come forward. I will not consent to see a friend of mine so vilely slandered."

Coroner Van Valkenburgh immediately wrote an order to have Mrs. Pattmore's body disinterred, and, also, a call for an inquest the following day. He had become very indignant at the idea of connecting his friend, Pattmore, with such a hideous crime; he, therefore, hurried over to tell Pattmore of the rumors, and of the prompt measures he had taken to prove their falsity. He drew Pattmore into a private room and told him all that he had heard and done. He expected that Pattmore would thank him heartily for his friendly action; but, instead, Pattmore's face turned very white, and he asked who it was that had spread the rumors. The coroner said that the sheriff and several prominent citizens had called upon him to investigate the rumors that were circulating at the hotels and on the street. Pattmore became very much excited when he heard this, and paced up and down in a nervous, irritable manner.

"Well," said Van Valkenburgh, "I will have the body

exhumed to-morrow, and when we have disproved the calumny, this scheme of your enemies will do you more good than harm."

"Yes," said Pattmore; "but my love for my wife is far above all other considerations. It is shocking to think that her body must be torn from the grave to refute the vile slanders of my political opponents. I do not know what course you usually pursue in such cases, but I would not, for the world, have her remains exposed to the gaze of a cruel, heartless crowd of strangers."

Mr. Pattmore's feelings quite overcame him, at the thought of such desecration, and he wept.

"I'll take care of that," said the sympathizing coroner; "I will have Dr. Forsythe make the examination, and his testimony will be sufficient for the jury."

"Well, I shall be satisfied with any arrangements you may make," said Pattmore. "I hope a good jury will be summoned; I do not wish my wife's body to be examined by a lot of curiosity seekers."

"Your wishes shall be attended to," replied the coroner. "I know who are your friends and I will summon no one else to sit on the jury."

"Van Valkenburgh," exclaimed Pattmore, seizing the coroner's hand, "I am your friend for life!"

He then led the way to the bar-room and invited the coroner to drink.

Miller was standing in the bar-room as the coroner and Pattmore passed, and noticing a haggard, pallid expression on the latter's face, he stepped up and said:

"Why, what's the matter Pattmore? Has anything gone wrong with you?"

"No, Mr. Miller, nothing very serious. Some of my enemies have started a story that I am responsible for my wife's death; but, of course, there is not a word of truth in it. The coroner has taken the matter in charge, and his verdict will soon set at rest these scandalous lies. There is nothing too sacred for these political harpies and ghouls: they literally have dragged the loved dead from the grave in the hope of injuring my reputation. Well, time will show my innocence."

So saying, Pattmore pressed Miller's hand warmly, as if overcome with emotion, and passed into the office. Mr. Green and Mr. Knox were watching him, and when he went up stairs, he was followed by Knox, who saw him go into his room. Knox immediately came down stairs and passed across the street to a corner where I had agreed to wait for him. Having heard his report I said:

"Mr. Knox, you are a stranger here, so you had better go back to see what Pattmore is doing. You can stumble into his room, as if you had mistaken it for your own. Be quick!" I added, as he started, "for we must keep watch of him every minute until the inquest has been held."

"Knox rushed into the hotel, ran up stairs and hastily entered Pattmore's room, where he found Pattmore writing a letter.

"Oh! I beg pardon," said Knox, "I have mistaken the room," and so saying, he withdrew and returned to me.

"So he is writing a letter, is he?" said I. "We must learn the contents of that letter, and I have not a minute to lose. Knox, find Green and Miller and bring them over here at once. Thank goodness, it is getting so dark that we shall not be noticed."

Knox was off like a shot, and in a very few minutes all my men were with me.

"Green," I said, "go to your hotel, pay your bill, and proceed to the Pattmore House. When you register your name, you must hail the clerk as an old acquaintance. This will be an easy matter, as hotel clerks are known by hundreds of people. Miller, you must be in the office at the same time, and you must both remain there until Pattmore puts his letter in the mail-box. Then, Green you must ask the clerk out to take a drink, and while you are gone, Miller must get possession of the letter. When you have secured it, come over to the Globe Hotel, where I am stopping."

Green hurried off to the Clarendon House to get his carpet-bag, and Miller returned to the Pattmore House. I also sent Knox to watch Pattmore, and to follow him wherever he might go, until he retired for the night.

Soon after Miller reached the office, Pattmore came down stairs with a letter, which Miller carefully scrutinized, so as to be able to recognize it among a group of others.

"Has the mail for the West closed yet?" asked Pattmore.

"No," replied the clerk, "there is still about an hour to spare."

Pattmore then dropped his letter into the mail-box and went out. At this moment Green stepped up to the desk, registered his name, and asked for a room. As the clerk was attending to his room and baggage, Green

"As soon as the clerk had left the office, Miller quietly extracted Pattmore's letter from the box."—Page 157.

looked intently at him, as if trying to recall his name. Then, stepping forward, he said, cordially:

"Why, how are you? When did you come here? Let me see; the last time I saw you was at a hotel in Buffalo, wasn't it?"

This was a lucky guess, for the clerk replied:

"Havn't you seen me since then? Why, I left there over a year ago."

"Well, I'm right glad to see you again," said Green; "step into the bar-room and take a 'smile' with me."

"I can't very well leave the office just now," said the clerk.

"Oh, yes you can," said Green; "your friend there will look after the office for a few minutes; come along."

"Wait here until I come back, will you?" the clerk asked Miller, as he went off with Green.

As soon as the clerk had left the office, Miller quietly extracted Pattmore's letter from the box. He had marked its appearance so well that he only needed one glance to identify it, and he secured it so quickly that none of the crowd outside the desk noticed any movement on his part. In a few minutes the clerk returned to the desk, and Miller lounged out into the bar-room, whence he hurried over to meet me at the Globe Hotel. He there gave me the letter, which was addressed:

"Mrs. Annie Thayer,
"Chicago,
"Illinois."

I carefully opened it by a simple process, which did not leave any evidence that the envelope had been tampered with. The letter began: "My own dear Annie," and the writer went on to caution Mrs. Thayer that she must not be alarmed at the news he was about to tell her. He said that some of his enemies had started a report that he had poisoned his late wife. He had no doubt that the Whig newspapers would spread and magnify these reports; still, he had no fears that they would be of any permanent injury to him, since his friend, coroner Van Valkenburgh, had agreed to hold an inquest, and there would be no difficulty in proving his innocence. He begged her to excuse the haste and brevity of the note, as he only had time to dash off a few lines to assure her that all was well, and to warn her not to become alarmed at anything she might see in the newspapers. The letter was signed: "Ever your loving and devoted husband, ALONZO PATTMORE."

"Well, this is certainly strange," I meditated. "Her 'devoted *husband*,' eh? How can that be? He has had no opportunity to marry her since his wife died; hence, unless he committed bigamy, this title of 'husband' is only assumed in anticipation; yet Mrs. Thayer is, undoubtedly, beautiful and winning, and she may have induced him to ease her conscience by a form of marriage, even while his legal wife still lived. I must look into this more closely on my return to Chicago."

I then re-sealed the letter and gave it back to Mr. Miller, with instructions to return to the hotel and keep a general watch on all that went on. He was not to mail the letter until early the next morning. As Miller went out Knox came in.

"Well, Knox, what news?" I asked.

"Mr. Pattmore has gone away in a hack," replied Knox, breathlessly.

"What direction did he take?"

"He drove off at a rapid rate toward the southern part of the town, and I could not keep up, nor get on behind. I took the number of the hack, though," answered Knox.

"That was right," I remarked, as Knox paused to get his breath.

"It was number fifty-two, and the driver seemed to be an Irishman. He looked like a genial, half-grown, young fellow, and I do not think I shall have any difficulty in pumping him when he returns, as I know where his stand is."

"Right again," I exclaimed. "Now you had better wait around there until the hack returns; then get into conversation with the driver, and ask him to take a drink in the nearest saloon; while you are talking with him, you can easily learn where Pattmore went."

It was ten o'clock when Knox left me, and, as I was greatly fatigued, I went to bed immediately. Shortly after midnight, Knox again awoke me.

"What news?" I asked, starting up. "Did you succeed in learning anything from the hackman?"

"Yes," replied Knox; "he returned a little before eleven o'clock, and I asked him whether he knew where there were any young ladies I could visit. He said that he knew several places. I then asked him to take a drink while we talked about it. I said, I judged, from his appearance, that he was just the young fellow who could take me where I wanted to go; that I was crossing the street to employ him in the early part of the evening, when he was taken by another gentleman, who probably went to the same kind of a place that I wanted to find. This had confirmed my opinion of the hackman, so I had decided to await his return. 'By the way,' I added, 'was I right about that gentleman?' The driver laughed loudly, and said that that was Mr. Pattmore, and that he did not go to such places. He went on to say that Mr. Pattmore's wife had been dead only a few days, and he supposed that Mr. Pattmore had gone out to pay the grave-digger, since his visit had been made to that individual at the graveyard gate."

"Did the boy say whether Pattmore saw the grave-digger?" I asked.

"Yes," continued Knox; "I pumped out all that the young fellow knew. The grave-digger lives in a little shanty close by the graveyard, and, on arriving there, Pattmore called the fellow to one side, and conversed with him in a low tone for some time. He then paid him some money, entered the hack, and told the boy to drive straight back to the Pattmore House, where Pattmore discharged the hackman. I drew this information out of the boy very easily, without appearing to take any special interest in the story. I then told him to drive me to some quiet house where I could meet some young ladies. He took me to a place near here, and I paid him off immediately, saying that I should spend the night there. As soon as he was out of sight, I came straight here, without going into the house at all."

"By Jove!" I exclaimed, "we shall have some rough work to-night, and we must be quick, too. Go over to the Pattmore House, find out from the register what room

Green is in, and wake him up as soon as possible. Tell him to come here, being careful that no one notices him, and to be sure to bring his pistols. You have yours, have you not, Mr. Knox?"

"Yes; do you expect to need them?"

"It is quite possible, as we shall have some risky work to-night. I will meet you outside, and you must tell Green to prepare for a march. Luckily we are all good walkers.

Knox hurried away, and, in a short time, both of my detectives joined me in the street. We then hired a hack and drove to within half a mile of the graveyard, where I paid off the hackman, and we entered the grounds of a residence, standing some distance back from the road. My object in entering these grounds, was to make the hackman believe we were stopping there; otherwise, his curiosity would have been excited as to my reasons for going into the country at that hour of the night. As soon as the hack was out of sight, we returned to the highway, and, after a brisk walk, we reached the graveyard.

CHAPTER V.

THE resting places of the dead are localities which I do not much care to visit in the night. In the day time it is different; there is a holy calm about a cemetery then which impresses me with a feeling of rest, and I can really enjoy an hour or two in quiet contemplation of the monuments and humble head-stones of a large burial ground. But in the night, even the least superstitious person in the world will be awed by the solemnity pervading our cities of the dead, and will quicken his pace as the wind rustles mournfully through the shrubbery. I never should care to go into a grave-yard at night, as a matter of choice; but business is business, and must be transacted, no matter how unpleasant the surroundings may be.

The first difficulty I encountered on entering the Greenville cemetery, was, that I did not know where Mrs. Pattmore's grave was located. We therefore separated to the distance of about one hundred yards, and advanced through the underbrush across the grounds. We arranged, before starting, to meet at a certain tall tree, which stood up against the sky in the dim starlight. Green had gone only a few rods when he came upon three men. Their smoky lantern threw a ghastly light upon their work, and they were so busily engaged in digging that they did not notice him. He quickly withdrew and hurried after me. It was some time after he overtook me before we could find Knox, but we finally met and returned to the place where the body-snatchers were at work. It was evident that they were professionals, for they had worked so rapidly as to have nearly succeeded in getting the coffin out of the grave.

A thrill of horror even now goes through me as I think of that night; the white tomb-stones stood forth among the foliage, by which they were surrounded, like sheeted ghosts, and the waving leaves gave them the appearance of weird shapes in fantastic motion. The light of the lantern feebly glimmered in one direction, and the body-snatchers flitted about like restless ghouls preparing for a horrible banquet. We approached as quietly as possible, and, on emerging from the cover of a copse of hazel bushes, we made a general rush forward. The ghouls were too quick for us, however, and they ran away at a break-neck speed which we did not dare to imitate. They had the great advantage of knowing every foot of the ground, while we were continually obliged to dodge around some obstruction. First, Knox stumbled headlong over a low grave, and then I became entangled in some trailing vines. As I regained my feet, I saw Green rising from an encounter with a chain which had tripped him, and we simultaneously abandoned the chase. It was clearly useless to follow them further, but we fired at them with our revolvers in the hope of frightening them into a surrender. One of them instantly stopped, returned our fire, and then continued his flight. This satisfied me that they were old hands at the business of grave-robbing, and that they were not to be scared by long-range pistol practice. After watching for a couple of hours, I returned with my men to the city, being convinced that the body-snatchers would not make another attempt to rob the grave. As I walked back, I tried to account, in my own mind, for this new move of Pattmore. I could not see the advantage to be gained by the removal of Mrs. Pattmore's body, and I retired to rest with that problem still unsolved.

Being greatly fatigued, it was eight o'clock next morning before I awoke. While I was at breakfast Mr. Miller came in, but he had nothing to report, except that Pattmore seemed greatly troubled, and looked very haggard. I ordered Miller to watch Pattmore closely, and to engage him in conversation as much as possible. I then went in search of Sheriff Tomlinson, whom I soon found. Believing him to be a thoroughly trustworthy man, I related to him all that had occurred the night before. He was much astonished at my story, and said that he was sorry I had not asked him to accompany me, as he knew the graveyard well. If the body-snatchers had been caught, they might have been able to give very important testimony at the inquest. Pattmore might have been held to appear before the grand jury on their testimony alone.

"Yes," I replied; "no one regrets their escape more than I do; but I am almost equally annoyed by the fact that I cannot reach a satisfactory conclusion as to Pattmore's motive in having his wife's body carried off. Of course, if the coroner's men should have found the body gone, every one would suspect Pattmore of having had it removed. However, I propose to solve the mystery in some way. By the way, Mr. Tomlinson, when do you expect the body to arrive?"

"It will be here by eleven o'clock, and the men having it in charge, will take it directly to Coroner Van Valkenburgh's office."

"I suppose he will impanel a jury," I remarked.

"Certainly," the sheriff replied; "and it would be well for you to be present to watch the proceedings. Pattmore must be made to face the music in some way."

Accordingly, I watched the coroner's office until I saw the hearse arrive, and, when the coffin was carried in, I followed it. The coroner's assistants reported that some body-snatchers had been at work, and had attempted to steal Mrs. Pattmore's body, having succeeded in getting the coffin nearly out of the grave; but they had evidently been interrupted, as they had left all their tools behind, and had not tried to open the coffin. They had been more successful in another case, however; the body of a woman had been taken from a grave in the Potter's Field, (which was devoted to paupers, etc.) and had been carried to a spot near Mrs. Pattmore's grave. The supposition was that the robbers, wishing to procure female subjects for dissection, had chosen those two graves as containing the bodies of persons who had most recently died.

On hearing this story, I saw through the trick at a glance. The sheriff was in the office, and I beckoned to him to join me outside.

"Mr. Tomlinson," I said, "I wish you to send a man to the graveyard to learn the name of the other woman, whose body was found; get a description of her age, height, size, and general appearance, as I feel sure that

Pattmore's intention was, to substitute her body for that of his wife."

"By Jupiter! that's so!" exclaimed Mr. Tomlinson; "but I should never have thought of that. I will attend to your request myself, while you can remain here to watch the proceedings before the coroner. I will go to the cemetery and make a thorough investigation. It is my duty to become acquainted with all the facts in the case," and he started off, accompanied by Mr. Green, whom I sent with him.

In a short time, Pattmore walked into the office and sat down. He wore a martyr-like expression, and, though he controlled his feelings sufficiently to appear outwardly calm, I could see that, inwardly, he was racked with fear and nervousness.

The coroner hastily impaneled a jury, consisting wholly of Pattmore's personal and political friends. The coffin was then opened, as a matter of form, and the jury merely looked at the rapidly decaying corpse. Pattmore refused to look at the body, on the ground that he did not wish to mar the sweet memories of his beloved wife's features, which he had seen only in the flush of life and beauty, even by a glance at her merely mortal remains in their present condition.

Dr. Forsythe testified that he had attended the late Mrs. Pattmore in her last illness, and that dysentery was the cause of her death. He was corroborated by another physician who had been in consultation with Dr. Forsythe during the last day or two of the patient's life. As no other witnesses were called, the jury immediately returned a verdict that Mrs. Pattmore's death had resulted from natural causes; namely, dysentery.

I was watching Pattmore closely during the interval before the verdict was delivered, and I saw plainly that, in spite of the farcical character of the inquest, he was in a state of nervous dread lest something unforeseen should occur to reveal his criminality. When the verdict was read, an expression of relief and triumph came into his face, and he received the congratulations of his friends like a man who had just escaped a great danger. I had too little evidence to warrant me in showing my hand at that time, by accusing him in person; nevertheless, I was satisfied of his guilt, and I decided to use other means to bring him to justice.

In about an hour, Sheriff Tomlinson returned from the graveyard, with Mr. Wells and Mr. Green. They had made notes of the condition in which they had found Mrs. Pattmore's grave, and they had written out a full description of the other corpse found near by. The body was that of a woman of about the same size, age, and general appearance as Mrs. Pattmore.

I had heard of an eminent physician in Greenville, named Dr. Stuart. On inquiring for him, Mr. Tomlinson took me to the doctor's office and introduced me. He was a man of great ability, and he had a high reputation throughout the West as a scientific analytical chemist.

I at once laid the facts in the Pattmore case before him, and said that I wished him to analyze carefully the contents of the stomach and bowels of the late Mrs. Pattmore, in order to determine whether she had been poisoned. I said that it was a difficult case to undertake, owing to Pattmore's political influence; but I felt sure that a thorough investigation would establish his guilt beyond question.

The Doctor replied that, under most circumstances, he should hardly feel inclined to comply with such a request, since he had no right to make such an analysis, unless he had the consent of the relatives of the deceased; or, upon the coroner's order. Still, he had a natural desire for fair play, and the facts which I had presented to him seemed to point toward the possibility that a foul crime had been committed; hence, he would perform the analysis, provided that his action should never be made known to any one, until he should be called upon to testify in court. Of course, if no trace of poison should be found, the theory of death by that means would have to be abandoned, and his connection with the affair need never be disclosed.

"I have never met you before, Mr. Pinkerton," concluded Dr. Stuart, "but your reputation is well known to me, and I feel sure that you would not have made this request unless there were strong reasons for such action. I have full confidence in you, and I will give you all the aid in my power. Where is Mrs. Pattmore's body now?"

"It is in the coroner's office," I replied, "and it will be taken back to the grave in about an hour."

"Well, Mr. Pinkerton, can't you obtain possession of it in some way? I shall only want it for a short time."

"That is what puzzles me," I replied; "I am afraid Pattmore will follow the body to the grave."

"Then, if he should do so, can't you get two men who

know how to handle a shovel quickly, to disinter it a second time?" asked the Doctor.

"Yes; I will take two of my own men," I said; "I can trust them more than any one else."

"Oh, nonsense!" exclaimed the Doctor, laughing, "you can do better than that. You had better offer the regular grave-diggers ten dollars to leave the body a short time in your possession before burying it; or, if Pattmore should insist upon seeing it buried, they can easily disinter it for you, and it will take me only a short time to remove the intestines. I shall then seal them up for the present, as I am too busy to make the analysis just now; but when I shall have finished my present work, I will take up this case. You can depend upon hearing from me at the earliest possible moment."

It was then arranged that Mr. Wells and sheriff Tomlinson should be present to witness the removal of the bowels from Mrs. Pattmore's body; the sheriff further decided to give an official order for the analysis, so as to protect Dr. Stuart in case of any accident. If any signs of poison were found, the Doctor's charges would be paid by the county; otherwise I should be responsible for the amount. I then went out to see the grave-diggers, and used such convincing arguments that they willingly agreed to disinter the body. My arguments were brief, but cogent, and were presented to them about in the following way:

"Mr. Grave-digger, you look like a man of discretion, who knows how to open his hands and shut his mouth. I wish to obtain the body of the late Mrs. Pattmore for a short time. I will give you several excellent reasons why you will be willing to let me have it. In the first place, I will give you twenty-five dollars for the job; secondly, ———"

"Wa-al, I guess you needn't go any furder," drawled the grave-digger, with a knowing wink; "twenty-five o' them reasons are enough for me; so just tell me where you want the body, and I'll see that it's forthcoming."

I have always found that half the argument may be dispensed with if the matter is only *presented in the proper light*.

In accordance with the agreement, therefore, the body was again taken from the grave in the presence of Mr. Wells, Sheriff Tomlinson, Dr. Stuart, my detectives, and myself; the necessary parts were removed by the Doctor, and the body was re-buried; finally, the Doctor placed the portions which had been removed in a jar of alcohol, and it was then sealed up to await the Doctor's analysis.

Of one thing I felt certain; and that was, that the regular grave-diggers and the body-snatchers of the night before were the same persons; hence, I feared that they might give Pattmore information of our proceedings. I communicated my opinion to the Sheriff, and suggested that a slight hint from him might induce the men to keep silence for their own protection. Accordingly he spoke to them about the occurrence of the previous night, and said that for the present he did not intend to make any investigation to learn who were the body-snatchers on that occasion.

"But," he added, significantly, "if I ever discover that Mr. Pattmore, or any one else, has been informed of this action which I have just taken, I shall consider it my duty as Sheriff, to bring to punishment immediately the men who attempted to rob this grave last night—*and I don't think I shall have any trouble in finding them.*"

While returning to the city, I impressed upon Sheriff Tomlinson the necessity of procuring all the evidence that could be reached relative to Mrs. Pattmore's death. I asked him particularly to find the nurses who attended her, and to learn all that they could tell about the symptoms of the patient; the kind and amount of medicines administered; the effect of the doses; and, in general, all the particulars of Mrs. Pattmore's illness and death. The Sheriff promised to do all in his power, and Mr. Wells also agreed to give his assistance in bringing out the whole truth.

On arriving at the Globe Hotel I met Miller, who gave me a copy of a letter which Pattmore had written to Mrs. Thayer, as soon as the coroner's jury had given their verdict. The letter contained a brief account of the inquest and the finding of the jury. It said that she could understand his feelings of great relief that all had turned out so well for him. The letter was signed, as in the former case, "Your loving husband."

Mr. Miller said that Pattmore's manner had wholly changed since the close of the inquest; before he had been morose and irritable; now he was all vivacity and good spirits. One of his first acts, after the verdict had been given, was to write the above-mentioned letter, which Miller had secured as before. Having taken a copy of it, Miller had mailed it in the general post-office.

"You have done very well, Mr. Miller," I said, "and I

wish you to remain here to watch Pattmore's movements and intercept his letters. I shall return to Chicago to-night, and you must inform me by telegraph if Pattmore leaves here."

Having completed all my arrangements, I returned to Chicago, taking Knox and Green with me.

CHAPTER VI.

MY first action, on reaching my office, was to send for Mrs. Kate Warne, the Superintendent of the Female Department of my force. She made a full report of all the work in her charge during my absence, and brought up among other cases, that of Captain Sumner.

"Miss Seaton," said Mrs. Warne, "reports that she has progressed somewhat toward an intimacy with Mrs. Thayer, but that she has learned very little except by observation. Mrs. Thayer seems to be greatly troubled at times, but she is very reserved, and does not appear anxious to make any one her confidant. She goes to the post-office regularly twice a day, but she rarely goes anywhere else. Once she went to a druggist's store, but, being unable to get what she wanted, she entered another one and purchased a small package."

"Has Miss Seaton been able to examine any of Mrs. Thayer's trunks or bureau drawers?" I asked.

"Only once," replied Mrs. Warne; "she succeeded in getting into one of her trunks, and there found an immense quantity of letters signed 'Alonzo Pattmore,' some of them dating back several years."

"Were they long, sentimental and — in short, were they to be classed under the head of love letters?" I asked, with a smile.

"Yes; Miss Seaton so reports them."

"Well," I said, "let her continue to watch Mrs. Thayer, and to seek to win the latter's confidence. By the way, what kind of books does Mrs. Thayer read?"

"Oh! anything that is romantic."

"Then, tell Miss Seaton to get 'Eugene Aram' and read it. She can make such allusions to it as will make Mrs. Thayer wish to read it too. The effect of the story on her mind will, perhaps, prepare her for the train of thoughts which I wish to excite in her."

"Oh! that reminds me," said Mrs. Warne, "Mrs. Thayer complains that she sleeps very poorly, and dreams a great deal. She has been wondering whether she talks in her sleep."

At this moment, one of my clerks entered and said that Captain Sumner wished to see me. I immediately sent word that he could come into my private office; at the same time, I requested Mrs. Warne to step into the next room for a few minutes, as I should need her, as soon as the Captain had gone. When the Captain entered, I was busily engaged in examining some papers, and I greeted him as if he were an old friend whom I had not seen for months.

"Why, how are you, Captain Sumner?" I said, shaking his hand, warmly. "I am delighted to see you."

"I'm pretty well," he replied; "but have you heard the news?"

"No; what news?"

"Read that," he said, handing me the Greenville *Advocate*, and pointing to an account of the inquest on Mrs. Pattmore's body.

The paper contained a full report of the coroner's proceedings, and an editorial on the subject. The editor spoke in the highest terms of Pattmore, and congratulated him on his triumphant vindication. I read all that the *Advocate* contained relative to the case, and then remarked:

"I wonder who started that investigation."

"I can't imagine," replied the Captain; "though, as the paper says, the story might have been originated by his enemies, for mere political effect."

"Yes; that is possible," I replied; "but there was no use in attempting anything of that kind. The result must have strengthened him, even among his opponents."

"I am afraid so, too," said the Captain. "We shall have a hard time in obtaining any proofs of his guilt, now that he is so popular."

I saw that the Captain did not suspect that I had been connected, in any way, with the Greenville inquest; I therefore, changed the subject.

"Well, it will all come out right, if you have patience. How is Mrs. Thayer?"

"Not at all well," he replied; "she is very restless, and she complains of being nervous; besides, she is more reserved with me than ever. Don't you think I had better try to induce her to go home with me? I should feel more comfortable if she were on the farm in Connecticut, as she would then be out of Pattmore's power. Sometimes I think there is no use in trying to reform her; for, she seems so infatuated with that man that I only wonder she has not run away with him before now. I know that she will marry him at the first opportunity."

"We must prevent that," I replied; "for the present, I think she had better remain here."

I then asked the Captain to excuse me a moment, and, stepping into the next room, I called my stenographer to the door; by leaving the door ajar, the conversation between the Captain and myself could be easily heard in the next room. The short-hand writer, therefore, was able to take down everything that was said. Returning to the Captain, I commenced a friendly chat, in the course of which, I led him on to talk about his family. I especially desired to draw out the particulars of Annie's history, and the honest old gentleman talked so freely that I obtained a very full account of all that he knew about her. In the conversation which we had about his own affairs, the Captain gave me the following story to account for the fact that he was an old bachelor:

"It seems somewhat strange," he said, "that I am unmarried, as I have always been a great admirer of the fair sex; but, the fact is, I had one strong affection, and that has lasted me all my life. The last time I was with her, she promised to be my wife, and we pledged ourselves to be eternally faithful to each other. I sailed for Singapore the next day, and, on my return, I was to lead her to the altar. I felt that I had secured a prize far beyond my merits, for she seemed to be superior to me in every way. The days dragged along slowly and wearily, while on the voyage; but, at length, we returned to New York. I immediately hurried up from the landing-place, all impatient to see my sweetheart. As I passed up the dock, I met an old acquaintance.

"'Where away so fast?' he asked, as he stopped me.

"'I am going to see Miss Curtis,' I replied.

"'Why, she married a rich banker, six months ago,' he said.

"'Oh! did she?' I exclaimed; 'I am glad she was so fortunate.'

"Then I returned aboard ship, feeling completely crushed. Since that time I have never paid attention to any other woman, for I can never forget her. Once afterward I met her on Broadway, on her way to her carriage. She nodded carelessly, with a 'How d'ye do, John?' and was quickly whirled away out of my sight. I have never heard from her since then.

After the Captain had told me everything about Annie and himself that he could recollect, I asked him to excuse me, pleading an important engagement at that hour. As soon as he had gone, I requested my stenographer to write out his notes in long hand as quickly as possible, and I returned to consult with my female superintendent.

"Mrs. Warne," I said, "we shall have a difficult task in working upon Mrs. Thayer; she seems to be very reticent and wary. I have decided to attack the superstitious side of her nature, which seems to be her weakest point; and, in order to do so successfully, I shall need your services. How do you think you would succeed as a fortune-teller?"

"A fortune-teller!" she exclaimed, laughingly; "that is certainly a new *role* ; however, I think I might learn to take the part after a few lessons."

"Yes," I replied, "the tricks of the trade are easily

learned. Here is a book which explains all the secrets of the profession. It is called 'The Mysteries of Magic and the Wonders of Astrology; by Dr. Roback.' You can take it to read at your leisure; but, after all, the costume and make-up are the principal things necessary. You will be obliged to trust largely to your own judgment and tact in working upon Mrs. Thayer's feelings. I suppose she has some vague ideas about astrology, etc., but I have no doubt of your ability to mystify her thoroughly. One thing is certain, Mrs. Warne, that we must have a fortune-teller of our own, and I do not know of any one so competent as yourself. I will rent an office for you near by, and the duties will interfere very little with your other work."

"I will undertake it," she said, decidedly, after a moment's thought; "I will make it a success, too, if you will give me my own way about it."

"All right," I answered; "success is all that I require."

Mrs. Warne then withdrew to make her preparations.

In a day or two I received a letter from Miller. He said that the talk over the inquest was gradually subsiding; that there were some few persons who were not fully satisfied with the manner of conducting the inquiry, but that the general effect had been favorable to Pattmore; that the latter had began to drink a great deal, though not enough to become intoxicated; that he, (Miller,) had been taken into Pattmore's confidence to a considerable extent; and that the latter had expressed an intention of going to Cincinnati to make a visit. In conclusion, he said that Pattmore was doing his utmost to appear cheerful, but that he looked very haggard, and seemed to be in great trouble.

Miss Seaton reported to Mrs. Warne the same day, that she was becoming more intimate with Mrs. Thayer, though the latter manifested no desire to take any one into her confidence. The day previous Mrs. Thayer had gone to the post-office, where she had received a letter, as usual. She had torn it open, as if very anxious to learn the news it contained for her, and had then crumpled it nervously in her hand, after reading it.

Miss Seaton also described a scene which had taken place that morning. Mrs. Thayer was in her room about eleven o'clock; soon afterward Miss Seaton went to the door and knocked. No answer being given, she went in quietly, intending to surprise Mrs. Thayer. She found the latter deeply absorbed in telling her own fortune with a pack of cards. Miss Seaton laughed pleasantly, and said:

"So you were telling your fortune, were you? Well, how did it come out?"

Mrs. Thayer looked somewhat confused at first, but she gathered up the cards mechanically, and said:

"I don't know how to tell my fortune; do you?"

"Yes, indeed, I used to be a splendid fortune-teller," replied Miss Seaton. "Let me try to tell your fortune."

She then shuffled the cards, dealt them in three piles, and turned up the last card, which happened to be the queen of hearts.

"Now let us see what your fortune *has* been, what it *is*, and what it *will* be," said Miss Seaton. "You are represented by the queen of hearts; this pile contains your past; that one your present; and the third your future."

So saying, she turned up the top card of each pile. By an odd coincidence the present and future were both clubs, the past being a diamond.

Miss Seaton said, gravely:

"Your past has been pleasant, but your future is unpromising."

"Yes, it is always so," replied Mrs. Thayer, despondently.

Then, as Miss Seaton was about to go on, Mrs. Thayer threw all the cards into a heap, saying:

"No, I don't want to hear any more; I shall have the same luck throughout; clubs always come to me."

"Have you always had such bad fortune?" asked Miss Seaton.

"Oh! no; only a few years ago, I used to be as happy as a bird; sorrow was unknown to me, and one enjoyment seemed to pass away only to be succeeded by another. Now I have nothing but trouble all the time."

"Your lot seems hard," remarked Miss Seaton, in a sympathizing tone; "probably you feel worse since your husband has been dead."

"Dead!" exclaimed Mrs. Thayer, springing up; then, recovering her presence of mind, she sat down, muttering: "yes, yes, of course, he's dead."

"What do you mean?" said Miss Seaton. "Is it long since he died?"

"I do not feel well to-day; and I shall not try to read my fortune again when I am so nervous," replied Mrs. Thayer, evading Miss Seaton's question.

Seeing that Mrs. Thayer wished to change the subject, Miss Seaton did not press her further. The two ladies remained together until dinner time, and Miss Seaton read a portion of "Eugene Aram" aloud. Mrs. Thayer became deeply interested in the book, and borrowed it to read.

Next morning I received a telegram from Miller, briefly stating that Pattmore had left Greenville. His destination was Chicago, though he had given out that he was going to Cincinnati.

I knew that he could not arrive that day, as the railroad connections were not promptly made at that time; but I instructed Mr. Knox and Mr. Green to be prepared to "shadow" him, on his arrival at the depot the next morning, and to keep upon his track constantly, while he remained in Chicago. I also sent word to Miss Seaton to make some pretense for calling upon Mrs. Thayer early in the forenoon, and to remain with her as long as possible. I knew that Pattmore would communicate with Mrs. Thayer immediately on his arrival, and my object was, to have some one to witness their meeting.

On entering my office early the next day, I was surprised to find Captain Sumner awaiting me, in a great state of excitement.

"That man has come here again, Mr. Pinkerton," he broke out, impetuously. "He came before breakfast and went straight to Annie's room. I called her to the door and expostulated with her, until she agreed to send him away as soon as possible. I then came here directly to inform you."

"Quite right, Captain," I replied; "there is nothing

like taking prompt action in such cases. You can return to the house now, and trust to me for the rest."

"But I'm afraid she will run away with that villain," said the Captain.

"Of course, we must prevent that," I replied; "I shall have a plan prepared, in case they attempt to run away together; but, I do not think Pattmore is quite ready yet for such a step. Keep your spirits up, Captain, and don't borrow trouble."

"I have all confidence in you, Mr. Pinkerton," he said as he went out; "but I shall be much happier when I am back on my farm."

According to instructions, Miss Seaton called on Mrs. Thayer, though she did not gain admittance to her room. When Mrs. Thayer opened the door, Miss Seaton saw that she had been crying, and that she was evidently much disturbed. She asked Miss Seaton to excuse her, as she had company from the East.

About noon Pattmore returned to his hotel, as the Captain would not permit him to dine at the boarding house. As Mrs. Thayer did not come down to dinner, Miss Seaton again visited her, and found her dressing to go out. She asked Miss Seaton to remain until she was dressed, but said that she was going out driving in the afternoon and to the theatre in the evening. In a short time, the Captain came in, and Miss Seaton retired. The Captain asked Mrs. Thayer what she meant by breaking her promises not to see Pattmore again.

She replied that Pattmore was a man she could not help loving; that she had tried her best to overcome her passion, but in vain; and that she could not break off the connection so abruptly, but that she would endeavor to do so gradually in the future. Then she kissed the Captain, saying that she was never so happy in her life, and that she was going out driving with Pattmore that afternoon. The Captain remonstrated with her without effect; and, seeing that he could not move her from her purpose, he came straight to my office to report.

Pattmore came again in the afternoon and took Mrs. Thayer out driving. She looked superb as she went off, having recovered entirely from her illness. She was in a perfect flutter of happiness and excitement, which gave her a brilliant color, and added to the brightness of her eyes. She was agitated by conflicting influences; on one side, was her brother, determined to separate her from her lover, and justly blaming her course; on the other, was Pattmore, claiming her love, and urging her to abandon her brother's protection.

They were gone about three hours, and, on their return, they seemed very complacent and much less excited than when they set out. In the evening, they went to the theatre together, being "shadowed" by Mr. Knox. He took a seat close behind them, in order to listen to their conversation; but he overheard nothing of any consequence.

Captain Sumner had a long talk with his sister next morning, in relation to their return to Connecticut. He begged her to go immediately, and thus escape from Pattmore's influence; but she opposed his wish, on the ground that she was too weak to make the journey. He then lost his temper, and replied that she was strong enough to go around to places of amusement with

Pattmore, and it was very strange that she could not travel slowly home. This show of anger on the Captain's part, caused her to commence crying, as she knew that he could not resist so powerful an appeal to his sympathy. The result equalled her anticipations. The Captain soon lost all his irritation and began to console her, as if she were a spoilt child; finally, she induced him to go driving with them that afternoon. The Captain told me afterward, that Pattmore behaved with great propriety during the drive, and that they did not seem to be so much in love with each other as he had supposed. I smiled inwardly at the old sailor's simplicity; for I noticed that they had gone out in an open barouche, (instead of a close carriage, such as they had used the day before,) and they had remained away only one hour, instead of three.

On their return from the drive, Pattmore and Annie went to Mrs. Thayer's sitting room, and the Captain went down town. At four o'clock, Miss Seaton knocked at Mrs. Thayer's door; but, receiving no answer, she tried to enter quietly. She found that the door was locked on the inside, however, and she was, therefore, obliged to withdraw to her own room to watch. It was six o'clock before Pattmore came out, having been nearly three hours in Mrs. Thayer's room with the door locked.

Mr. Knox "shadowed" Pattmore, on his departure from the boarding house, and saw him take the nine o'clock train for Greenville. I immediately notified Mr. Miller by telegraph, directing him to renew his intimacy with Pattmore, and to remain in Greenville until further orders.

CHAPTER VII.

MR. MILLER was not idle during the time that Pattmore was away. His first action was to learn who were the nurses attending Mrs. Pattmore in her last illness. One of them had left the city, but the other, being an old resident of Greenville, was soon found. She was quite an elderly woman, with no family except one daughter. The latter was a seamstress, and Mr. Miller soon made her acquaintance by employing her to make some shirts for him. He kept up friendly relations with them by taking both mother and daughter out riding occasionally in the summer evenings; and in various ways he ingratiated himself into the old lady's confidence. It was not long before he was able to draw out all the particulars of Mrs. Pattmore's illness.

He learned that when she first became seriously sick, Mr. Pattmore began to show a very tender solicitude for her health.

He even insisted upon preparing her medicine and giving it to her himself. Mrs. Pattmore, however, did not seem to appreciate his watchful care, for she told the nurse that she did not like to take her medicine from her husband; she also asked very particularly whether the medicine which she took was that which the doctor prescribed.

Mrs. Reed, the nurse, said that she did not like the effects of the medicine at all. It was put up in small yellow papers, and when Mrs. Pattmore took a dose of it she was always taken with violent vomiting; her bowels and stomach would become very hot, and the pain would be so severe as to cause her to scream terribly. Then Mr. Pattmore would give her a dose of another kind of medicine, which would soon relieve the patient and cause her to fall into a deep sleep.

When Dr. Forsythe called, Mrs. Pattmore always informed him very carefully about the effect of the medicine, but he treated it as a case of common occurrence, and said that those symptoms invariably accompanied an attack of dysentery. After the Doctor had gone, Mr. Pattmore would return to the room with the same medicine, and his wife would exclaim:

"Oh! has the Doctor ordered that horrid medicine again? I cannot stand it long. Oh! what shall I do?"

Then her husband would tell her that it pained him almost as much as herself to see her suffer so, and that he would willingly take it himself if he could thereby save her from pain; but she must recollect that she was very dangerously sick, and that a failure to obey the Doctor's instructions might prove fatal to her. Mrs. Pattmore would be too feeble to protest long, and she would take the medicine; the same symptoms as before would then result, and each day she seemed to grow weaker and weaker.

The day of Mrs. Pattmore's death the Doctor was unable to call; hence only Mr. Pattmore and Mrs. Reed were present when she died. Pattmore spoke very endearingly to his wife and tried to caress her, but she pushed him away, gave him one long, reproachful look, and fell back dead. Pattmore professed to be overcome with grief, and tears flowed down his cheeks, as he requested Mrs. Reed to arrange for the funeral, and to spare no expense. He stopped at the door as he was leaving the room and said:

"By the way, Mrs. Reed, if any one inquires about it, you can say that dysentery was the cause of my beloved wife's death."

Miller said that there was little doubt that Mrs. Reed suspected foul play in connection with Mrs. Pattmore's death; but she was a very discreet woman, and would not spread any story which she could not prove. It was only by very skillful management that he had been able to induce her to talk upon the subject at all. She knew that Pattmore was very popular, and that she would be speedily silenced if she attempted to suggest anything against his character; hence she preferred to keep her suspicions to herself.

On receiving this report from Miller, I sent him instructions to continue his acquaintance with Mrs. Reed, and to keep a close watch upon her movements, for it was possible that she, too, might be induced to go away. As she would be an important witness, it would be necessary not to lose sight of her. At the end of the week I received another report from Miller, stating that Pattmore had called a select meeting of his political supporters in the district, and had laid the plans for an energetic effort to obtain the Congressional nomination. Miller had been taken into their confidence, and he was working hard to secure the election of Pattmore delegates to the approaching convention. This gave him ample opportunity to become intimate with Pattmore, and he felt sure that the latter would not take any important steps without consulting him.

I was much pleased to hear this news, as it showed me that Pattmore was no longer in fear of detection; moreover, it satisfied me that politics would detain him in Greenville for some time, and there would be no immediate danger of his marriage with Mrs. Thayer. Having a prospect that he would not return to Chicago to interfere with my plan for some weeks, I decided to proceed with my attack on Mrs. Thayer's credulity and superstition. In the afternoon, therefore, I sent for Mrs. Warne, and asked whether she had secured rooms in which to play the part of a fortune-teller.

"Yes," she replied, "I have rented three rooms on Clark street, which are just suited for the purpose. There are two entrances, so that you can slip in at any time without being seen by my visitors."

"Well, you had better have them fitted up as soon as possible. I will drop in to look at them to-day."

"No," she answered, "I don't wish you to come until I have completed my preparations. The rooms are on the second floor, and have not been occupied for some time; hence they will need considerable cleaning. You are too busy to attend to the furnishing and arranging, so I will relieve you of all the trouble; only give me *carte-blanche* for the purpose of furnishing the rooms, and I know you will not regret it."

"All right," said I; "you have my permission to do as you please, and you can get whatever money you need from the cashier. All I ask is that everything be done in the best manner. When you are ready to begin operations let me know, so that I can have an audience with the great fortune-teller in advance of the general public."

During the next four days, nothing of any consequence occurred. The Captain reported that his sister was gaining so fast in health and strength that he thought she was able to go back to Connecticut. Of course, I was obliged to oppose the journey at that time, since I wished to bring Mrs. Thayer before my fortune-teller. Miss Seaton reported that she was on quite intimate terms with Mrs. Thayer; but the latter never talked about her own affairs. She wrote daily to Pattmore, and received daily letters in reply.

At length, Mrs. Warne reported that her temple of magic was in complete order, and that she would be ready to receive me that afternoon.

"Very well," I replied; "I will drop in to have my fortune told about three o'clock. Have you arranged it wholly to your own satisfaction?"

"Yes; it is nearly perfect."

"Whom have you engaged for an usher?" I inquired.

"You must not ask questions now," she answered, laughing. "I have taken more liberties than I ever dared to take before; but I think, when you consider the object to be gained, that you will be satisfied."

"Well, I hope your rooms are as mysterious as your answers would lead me to expect," said I. "However, I shall be there promptly at three o'clock, so I will restrain my curiosity for the present."

At the appointed hour, therefore, I called at the rooms,

where I was received by a young negro of the blackest type. He was dressed in full Turkish costume, and his actions gave me the impression that he was dumb. This black mute first ushered me into a very large front room, elegantly furnished in the style of a modern *salon*. Heavy curtains hung in graceful folds from richly gilded cornices, sufficiently obscuring the windows to prevent the strong glare of the afternoon sun from penetrating directly into the room; arm-chairs and sofas were plentifully scattered about, to accommodate the throng of persons who were expected to visit the fortune-teller; the walls were hung with engravings and paintings; and on the floor was a thick Brussels carpet, into which my feet sank noiselessly, as I walked about inspecting the pictures and furniture. After scanning the sable usher for a few minutes, I said:

"Now, if that color would wash off, I should feel sure of finding one of my office boys, named Jack Scott, underneath." The mute grinned responsively, and I saw that I had guessed correctly. "Well, Jack," I continued, "I don't think you need fear detection. Where is Mrs. Warne?"

Jack still remained mute; but he went into another room, and soon beckoned me to follow him. As I crossed the threshold, the door closed noiselessly behind me. It took me several seconds to accustom my eyes to the change in the light. Then I began to gather an idea of the surroundings, and my surprise at Mrs. Warne's success was equalled only by my admiration of her good taste and judgment.

The room was nearly square, but a large mirror, at the end opposite the entrance, gave a duplicate view of the whole; the shape of the mirror being that of a large doorway, the effect was to give an appearance of two rooms, instead of one. The walls and windows were hung with some dark colored material, which wholly shut out every ray of sunlight; but a soft, dim radiance was shed from five swinging lamps, one in each corner and the fifth in the centre of the room. These lamps were of bronzed silver, of Oriental patterns, and were all in motion; the corner lamps swinging back and forth toward the centre, and the centre one, swinging slowly around in a circle. On the walls, were hung several charts and mystic symbols, while the floor was covered with a close matting of white straw, upon which was painted the common representation of the signs of the zodiac. A number of small globes stood upon a low shelf in one corner, and on a table in the centre of the room was a large globe, standing on a chart. With the exception of one large easy-chair and a lounge, there were no other articles of furniture in the room. A pair of skeletons stood facing each other, one at each side of the mirror, and their ghastly appearance, duplicated in the mirror, added to the unnatural effect. Near the table was a small portable furnace upon which stood a, peculiarly shaped retort, and from this, issued a pungent, aromatic incense.

While I was examining the globe and chart, Mrs. Warne slipped into the room, through the folds of a curtain at one side of the mirror, and swept down toward me. I should hardly have known her, so great was her disguise; her face and hands were stained a clear olive, and her hair hung down in heavy masses to her waist; her dress was of rich material, trimmed with Oriental extravagance; the sleeves were large and flowing, and the skirt trailed over a yard. In her right hand she carried a small wand, around which two serpents twined. Her whole appearance was dignified and imposing. The light and atmosphere added to the general effect, and I felt wholly satisfied with Mrs. Warne's work.

"Well, Mrs. Warne," said I, "you have certainly made a great success; but I am afraid I shall not be so much pleased when the bills come in."

"Don't be very much alarmed on that score," replied Mrs. Warne. "I have been very economical. Many of the most expensive articles have been hired for the occasion, while the rest have been picked up cheap at auction sales. The expense, I assure you, will not be great."

"All right," I rejoined; "the Captain will have to foot the bill, whatever it may be; but, if we succeed in our object, he will not have any reason to regret the cost."

Mrs. Warne showed me the door through which she had entered, and asked me to seat myself behind the curtains. She then called her usher into the room, and conversed with him; though they spoke in low tones, I was able to hear every word. The door where I was sitting, was hung on noiseless hinges, and it led into the last room of the suite; from this room, another door opened on a hall leading to a pair of side stairs. I was thus able to reach my ambush without entering by the front way.

"Now, Mrs. Warne, nothing remains to be done but to advertise you thoroughly," I said, after I had inspected all her preparations.

"Very well," she replied; "but you must recollect that

I shall not be able to oversee all my general work, unless you make my office hours as a fortune-teller very short. Three hours will be the longest time I can spare daily."

I then returned to my office and wrote out the following advertisement:

THE GREAT ASIATIC SIBYL,

L. L. LUCILLE, the only living descendant of Hermes, the Egyptian, who has traveled through all the known parts of the world, now makes her first appearance in Chicago. She will cast the horoscope of all callers; will tell them the events of their past life, and reveal what the future has in store for them. She has cast the horoscope of
all the
crowned
heads of Eu-
rope, Asia, Africa,
and Oceanica; she will
cast the horoscope, or celes-
tial map, for the hour and moment of the inquiry for any visitor
with the same care, and by the same
method as that used in the case of the Sultan
of Turkey, and the Pacha of Trincomalee. She will remain only a short time in Chicago; hence the
SORROWFUL AND AFFLICTED,
who wish to know what the future has in store for them,

had better CALL AT ONCE.
She will tell
WHO LOVES YOU; WHO HATES YOU;
and who is trying to injure you.
She will show you
YOUR FUTURE HUSBAND OR WIFE.
L. L. LUCILLE is the
Seventh Daughter of
a Seventh Daughter.
She never fails to give satisfaction.
Visit her and learn your fate
Office hours—10 a. m. to 1 p. m.
Fee $10.00.
OFFICE AT THE TEMPLE OF MAGIC,
50 SOUTH CLARK STREET.

This advertisement was inserted in the daily newspapers for a week, and I also had a number of small handbills printed for distribution in the street. In this way Lucille's name was brought before the public very conspicuously. At that time the trade of fortune-telling was not so common as it is now, and those engaged in it rarely had the means to advertise themselves so extensively; hence Lucille's half column in the newspapers attracted an unusual amount of attention.

CHAPTER VIII.

THE next morning Miss Seaton called on Mrs. Thayer as usual, and found her eagerly reading Lucille's advertisement in one of the newspapers. Miss Seaton asked Mrs. Thayer whether she was ready to go out for their regular morning walk, and Mrs. Thayer soon prepared to accompany her. They first went to the post-office; and, as they walked away, after Mrs. Thayer had received a letter, they met a boy distributing hand-bills. They each took one and walked along slowly in order to read Lucille's glowing advertisement. Mrs. Thayer folded her bill up carefully and said:

"I wonder whether this woman can do what she claims; if I thought so, I would call on her myself."

"Well, I don't have much faith in these people, as a rule," replied Miss Seaton, "but it is a fact that some of them really have a strange and inexplicable power to foresee events. Whether it is a genuine science, or a mere application of general rules of physiognomy to the particular features of each visitor, I do not profess to say; but there is no doubt, I believe, that they have been very successful in reading the future for some people."

"I am so glad to hear you say that," said Mrs. Thayer, "for I was afraid that you would laugh at me. Now I have a real desire to see this woman, just to test her powers. The moment I read her advertisement in this morning's paper, I had a strong presentiment that she could help me out of my troubles, and I determined to visit her. See, here we are, right at the door, No. 50 Clark street. Won't you go up with me while I get my fortune told, Miss Seaton?"

"Oh, certainly; if you really wish to try your fortune, to-day is as good a time as any other."

They therefore ascended to Madam Lucille's rooms and rang a bell at the reception-room door. The sable usher immediately admitted them and asked them to be seated for a short time, as Madam was engaged at that moment. He then left them alone, while he went to inquire how soon they could have an audience with the great sibyl. Having told Mrs. Warne who her visitors were, the usher hurried over to my office and informed me. I instantly called my stenographer, and we proceeded quickly to the back room, where we took our seats behind the curtain.

A lady was already in Mrs. Warne's room, but she was easily dismissed with instructions to return next day. When she retired, Mrs. Thayer was admitted, and Miss Seaton wished to follow, but this could not be allowed, as only one could have an audience at a time. Mrs. Thayer entered the room with her veil down; and, what with her nervousness and the superstitious terror inspired by the weird appearance of the room, she was hardly able to walk to the visitor's chair. When she became somewhat accustomed to the peculiar light, she saw Madam Lucille standing beside the table. Her tall, commanding figure struck Mrs. Thayer with awe, and

Mrs. Warne already felt sure of drawing out everything that she knew.

"Come hither, my daughter," said Lucille, in a clear, sweet voice.

Mrs. Thayer advanced falteringly, and sank into the large chair which the sibyl pointed out.

"What would you know, my child?" continued Lucille. "State your errand quickly; as my time is short, to unfold the mysteries of the future. Like the Wandering Jew, I must forever advance upon my mission. What do you seek to know?"

Lucille's powerful mind, aided by her fantastic surroundings, had gained a complete ascendency over Mrs. Thayer's superstitious nature; in a voice trembling with emotion, she replied:

"I have come to learn my future."

"Then you must unveil; I can tell you nothing until I see your face," said Lucille.

Mrs. Thayer slowly removed her veil and sat motionless, regarding the fortune-teller as a frightened bird watches a snake.

"You wish to know your destiny, do you?" asked Lucille, gently. "Well, I can tell it, if the stars are propitious; but I must first look at your hand."

She paused and waved her wand with several mysterious gestures over Mrs. Thayer's head; then she swept forward and took her hand.

"Tell me the day and hour of your birth," continued Lucille.

"I was born about daybreak on the eighteenth of

October, 1816, replied Mrs. Thayer; "I cannot tell you the exact hour."

"That will be sufficiently accurate for the present," said Lucille; "though it may cause me much trouble in casting your horoscope."

Lucille continued to examine the lines of the hand, and presently commenced speaking in a low, but clear voice:

"Your parents are dead, and also one brother; your father passed through great dangers safely—ah! I see, he was a sailor. You have been surrounded by other sea-faring people; still, I cannot certainly tell what relationship they bore to you. I shall learn all when I cast your horoscope. Your father acquired moderate wealth, of which you have received your share; but you desire more, and you are not too scrupulous as to how you get it. Why, what means this?" she exclaimed, starting back and fixing a piercing glance on the cowering woman before her. "You are in danger! Yes; there is danger all about you, but it is impossible to tell now how it will end. There is a man in your trouble, who claims to love you; and there is a woman who comes between you. Ah! what is she doing!" she suddenly demanded in tragical tones, starting back with a look of terror in her eyes.

Mrs. Thayer fell back as if stabbed to the heart, and her whole attitude denoted guilty fear. Lucille, fearing that she would faint, handed her a glass of water, which soon revived her strength.

As soon as Mrs. Thayer had sufficiently recovered,

"*Death!*" shrieked Mrs. Thayer, and then she fell back lifeless."—Page 190.

Lucille again took her hand and carefully examined it; she then continued:

"I cannot do much now, but you must come again, when I have more time; then I will cast your horoscope, and will be able to tell you all you can wish to know——" Breaking off suddenly, she changed her tone and demanded imperiously: "Who is this woman? Is she his enemy, or yours? *Are you sure that man loves you?*"

"Oh! yes; I am sure he does," Mrs. Thayer replied, hastily.

"Then what is the trouble between you and this woman?" asked Lucille. "She is older than you, yet she constantly crosses your path." Then, closing her eyes, Lucille broke out passionately and rapidly, like a person in a trance: "Why does she act so? What is the matter with her? She is often interfering with you, but is always followed by that man; he must be her enemy. See! a shadow falls over her! What does it mean! She fades away and vanishes—*it must be death!*"

"Death!" shrieked Mrs. Thayer, and then she fell back lifeless.

Lucille did everything possible to revive her visitor, but it was some minutes before she recovered sufficiently to be able to stand alone. She finally joined Miss Seaton, but promised to call the next day to have her horoscope read. She left a fee of ten dollars for the prepayment of the labor which Lucille would be forced to perform in reading the stars. When Miss Seaton and Mrs. Thayer left the room, the latter was scarcely able to walk, so much was she agitated and alarmed. They reached their boarding house in safety, however, and Mrs. Thayer at once retired to her room.

A large crowd of visitors had already assembled in Madam Lucille's reception room, so that there seemed to be a fair prospect that all the expenses of the affair would be paid out of the fortune-teller's receipts. Indeed, from the very first, Mrs. Warne had a great many more callers than she could attend to; but, by granting each one a short interview on the first day, long enough to learn what information they desired, it was an easy matter to satisfy them all to an exceptional extent. I put two good detectives at work to find out everything possible about the parties making the inquiries, and Lucille was thus able to astonish them with the accuracy of her knowledge as to the past. Of course, she was at liberty to exercise her own judgment as to her predictions for the future, since no one could tell whether they would prove true or not.

When every one had gone, Mrs. Warne changed her dress and returned to my office, where we had a hearty laugh over the superstitious folly of the many ladies who had consulted her. She told me many amusing secrets, which her fair visitors had confided to her, and I learned that some of the most fashionable people in the city had invoked her aid. She was rather fatigued by her labors, however, as the weather was warm, and the atmosphere of her room, at times, became almost suffocating. She said that she had made an engagement to admit Mrs. Thayer the first one, the next morning.

"Very well," said I, "you have succeeded in startling her very much indeed, and to-morrow you will be able to do much more. Be careful, however, to warn her against informing any one else of what you have told her, until her whole future is determined. It will not do to have her alarm Pattmore."

"I will caution her particularly on that point," replied Mrs. Warne; "I think I understand pretty well about how far I can go without terrifying her too much. I will send for Miss Seaton, and learn how Mrs. Thayer has acted since visiting me."

In the afternoon, Captain Sumner came in and asked what steps I had taken in his case. I told him that I could not tell him what I had done, nor what I was doing; but he could rest assured that the best talent I had was employed in his behalf; if everything worked as I hoped, I should accomplish the object which he sought, inside of a month.

"Well," he replied, I should like to take Annie back to Springfield as soon as possible; for I fear that she is again losing her health, and for the last day or two, she has been quite ill. Yesterday she received a letter from Pattmore, which I tried to snatch from her; but she was too quick for me, and I obtained only a small part of it. Here it is," he continued, showing me the lower corner of a letter; "see how he signs himself."

I took the fragment and saw the same signature as that which Pattmore had used in his former letters: "Your affectionate husband." The Captain went on:

"My blood got up when I read this, and I told her that if she ever saw Pattmore again, I would shoot them both; that I would no longer permit her to disgrace our family. Then she also flew into a violent passion, and said that she loved Pattmore, and that he intended to marry her when he next came to Chicago. As usual, she finally succeeded in appeasing my anger, and she promised to leave Pattmore forever. I also agreed to make my will in her favor, and we thus became friends again. I may now be able to get her away, as she has promised to go as soon as she is able; but I can easily destroy my will, if she refuses to keep her promise. What do you think about it?"

"Well, it can't do much harm, I guess, for you are probably in no particular danger just now."

"Then I will make my will to-day. By-the-by, there is a great fortune-teller in town; have you seen her advertisement?"

"Yes," I replied; "but there is nothing unusual in that. You can find such people here at all times."

"I know that," said the Captain; "but they are generally mere humbugs, while this one appears to be of a different class. She has been in the East Indies, and the fortune-tellers there are not humbugs, as I know by experience. I shall go to see her to-morrow. I had my fortune told once by a Hindoo in Calcutta, and he was correct in every particular as far as he went."

After the Captain had gone away, I sent for Mrs. Warne and told her that she would receive a visit from the Captain next day, and that she could learn all about his past history by referring to the conversation which my stenographer had taken down some time before. I then looked over a report I had just received from Miller, who was still watching Pattmore in Greenville. There was little of importance in it except an account of a conversation between Miller and Pattmore, in which the latter said that he was staking everything upon the hope of getting the congressional nomination; if he should fail in that, he would not remain in Greenville, but would go to Kansas to live. Miller added that Pattmore received letters daily from Mrs. Thayer.

I immediately wrote to Miller to secure a copy of one of Mrs. Thayer's letters; and, if possible, to intercept every one of them. I felt confident that she would describe her visit to the fortune-teller in part, at least, and I was anxious to know how much she would reveal to him. Besides if he were disposed to be superstitious, he would probably be more or less affected by her account, and I might use the knowledge thus gained, to good advantage.

Late in the evening, Miss Seaton came in and told Mrs. Warne that Mrs. Thayer had been greatly agitated by her interview with Lucille; that she had shown great dejection and grief all the way home; and that she had immediately retired to her room, where she had thrown herself on the bed; that she had risen, late in the evening, and had written a very long letter, which she had asked Miss Seaton to put in the post-office for her, being too weak to go out herself. Of course, Miss Seaton gave the letter to Mrs. Warne, who immediately brought it to me. I opened it at once and hastily read it through. It began, "My dear husband," and went on to describe her visit to Lucille. She gave a full account of all that Lucille had said, and also related the effect which the fortune-teller's revelations had had upon her. She said significantly that Pattmore could understand how much she had been alarmed by the references to the woman who came between them, for the inference was that Lucille meant Mrs. Pattmore. However, she was going, she said, to have her full fortune told the following day, and she would write all about it in her next letter.

I had the letter copied and sent to the post-office in time for the first mail.

CHAPTER IX.

I HAD sent word to my New York correspondent to make a thorough search for Henry Thayer, as I wished to learn definitely whether he was alive or dead. By communicating with the London board of underwriters, my agent learned that Henry Thayer was in command of an English whaler in the South Sea. At the latest advices from him, he was nearly ready to sail for England, as he needed only a few more whales to complete his cargo. I received this information the morning after Mrs. Thayer's first visit to Lucille, and I communicated the news to Mrs. Warne at once, instructing her to make the best possible use of it in her coming interview with Mrs. Thayer.

Shortly before ten o'clock the next morning, I took my place behind the curtain. In a few minutes Mrs. Thayer and Miss Seaton arrived, and Mrs. Thayer was promptly admitted to Lucille's presence. She removed her veil and sank into the visitor's chair with an expression half of longing and half of dread. Again Lucille waved her snaky wand, and, as before, the room was filled with the fumes of burning incense. Lucille looked at Mrs. Thayer's face intently, and said:

"My child, I am pleased to see you; I have worked at your horoscope unremittingly, but it is not completed to my satisfaction. There is some peculiar influence about you which prevents a clear reading of your future. Even your past, though much of it is easily determined, seems obscured by strange inconsistencies—not to say impossibilities. Some of the results were so startling as to make it necessary for me to refuse to reveal them, until, by a second test, I can decide whether there was no mistake in the solution of certain calculations. To-night, therefore, I shall do what rarely is necessary in reading the horoscope of ordinary humans—I must invoke the aid of my progenitor and master, Hermes. It is a dreadful task; one for which I must nerve myself to meet the greatest dangers and the most frightful scenes; but I never shrink from the path of duty, and I have confidence that the sanctity of my mission will give me safe conduct, even through the hosts of demons who must be met before I can come face to face with the great Egyptian king."

Lucille spoke with a weird earnestness, and a far-away look in her eyes, as if she actually realized the presence of ghouls and goblins. Mrs. Thayer fairly shivered with terror, but said nothing, and Lucille continued:

"I wish I dared read the whole of the horoscope as it was divulged to me in the lone watches of last night; but I have decided to omit all those portions where there is a possibility that the malign spirits around you have misinterpreted your past and future. When you were younger, you passed your days in happiness; you were very handsome, and you could charm the hearts of men without difficulty. There has been with you frequently, during your past years, a man some years older than yourself. He appears to have been a sailor; and, though often away from you, he has always sought you out on his return. He loves you, and is undoubtedly your true friend; he is unmarried, yet he does not wish to make you his wife. He wears a peculiar ring which he obtained in the East Indies. He often consults this ring, and it informs him whether he is in danger or the reverse. You do not love this sailor as well as he loves you, and he wishes to remove you from the other man. I cannot understand the actions of the woman whom I mentioned yesterday; I cannot tell whether she is living or dead. The man you love has been with her; he gave her something in a spoon which she was forced to take. Ah! I see! it was a medicine, a white powder—and now begins the obscurity. Further on, I see that he visited you; you ran to meet him and plied him with caresses. If he were your husband it would partly clear away the cloud. Is it so?"

"Yes," Mrs. Thayer at length replied, "he is my husband."

"Well, that removes much of the uncertainty; this woman loved that man and wished to keep him away from you; he gave her a powder to make her sleep, so that he could escape from her."

Then, suddenly catching Mrs. Thayer's hand, Lucille glanced over it rapidly, and again closely examined the chart. Drawing back from Mrs. Thayer, she eyed her sternly and disapprovingly.

"Who is this other·man?" she asked; "he, too, is a sailor; he is handsome; he is brave; he is an officer; yes, he commands a ship. He has been much with you, but he is now far away. You loved him once, but now the other man has come between you." Then, pausing a moment, she broke forth rapidly and harshly: "Woman, you have tried to deceive me! This sea captain is your husband!"

Mrs. Thayer was only able to say, as she fell back, fainting:

"He is dead! he is ——"

Lucille soon revived her, and then asked whether she was strong enough to hear the remainder of her fortune. Mrs. Thayer signified her assent, and Lucille again examined the chart. She first said:

"You cannot deceive me; your husband is away at sea; is it not so?"

"He *was* my husband," said Mrs. Thayer, in a half audible voice; "but he went away several years ago, and I heard that he was dead. I had fallen in love with the other man, and, on hearing of my husband's death, I married the man I loved. It can't be possible that Henry is alive."

"Yes, he is," replied Lucille; "and I think he is about to return to seek for you; but the horoscope again becomes obscure. It is as I feared; the only means of learning the truth will be through the aid of the dread Hermes, whose power no demon can resist. To-morrow you shall learn all that my art can discover about your past and your future."

"But can you tell me no more than this to-day?" asked Mrs. Thayer, in a vexed tone. "You have given me only bad news. How long shall I live and be happy with my husband?"

"That man is not your husband, and you cannot long

live happily with him. As far as the cloud permits me to see, I can discern that something terrible is about to happen to him. You are in danger yourself; there seems to be a strange fatality attending your fate wherever it comes in contact with that man; it is especially gloomy when complicated by the presence of the other woman. As I have before told you, I cannot clearly see from this horoscope what will be your *absolute* future; but I can tell you this much: — and, woman, weigh well my words, for the spirit of prophecy is strong within me — your future is dependent upon your present decision. Fate is unchangeable, and neither seer nor sibyl can alter its least decree; but it is sometimes permitted to us to determine the *contingent* future of a person and no more. We then say, thus and thus has been the past; the future may be thus, or it may be so; one course of conduct now, will lead to *this* result; the other will lead to *that.* Yours is such a horoscope; and, even with the aid of my mighty master, I cannot expect to do anything more than to learn definitely the two alternatives which are to be presented to you, and the consequence of your decision each way. To-morrow I will see you again at an early hour, and will tell you all I have learned during the night."

"Can you tell me no more now?" demanded Mrs. Thayer, impatiently. "Is it then true that my first husband is alive?"

"It is true," replied Lucille; "and he is at present commanding a ship far away in the South Sea, which is the reason why you could not find him."

"How do you know that I ever looked for him?" said Mrs. Thayer, languidly.

"No; you did not look for him; but the other sailor who loves you, made inquiries for a long time. I see him plainer now; he must be your brother."

Mrs. Thayer had been very much awed by the imposing manners of Lucille, and by the mystic surroundings in which she was placed. She was now quite in Lucille's power, and I should have proceeded to force her to reveal the truth about Pattmore's crime, had she been stronger physically; but I was afraid to test her endurance too far in one day. I had arranged a series of simple signals, which would not attract the attention of any one but Lucille, and I therefore signalled to her that she might close the interview. Mrs. Thayer lifted her head to look at Lucille a few moments after the latter had spoken of her brother, and said:

"You are the strangest woman I have ever met. You have told me things which I believed were known only by myself. All that you have said is the truth; but you do not tell me enough. I wish to know what I must do to make amends for all the wrong I have done. I have been very wicked, I know."

"If you really wish to do right, there is still a prospect that you may be happy. My duty is to show you that you are doing wrong, and to help you to change your course of action."

"Will you not tell me about my—"

Mrs. Thayer could not complete the sentence, but she evidently meant Pattmore, so Lucille said:

"Yes, my child; I will tell you all to-morrow; but I

think you are unable to bear more at present. I will point out two paths, and will show you where each one of them leads: then, if you wish, I will give you my advice; after that, all will depend upon yourself. You can be happy again, if you decide to follow my counsel."

"Indeed, I will try to do so," replied Mrs. Thayer. "I have suffered myself to be led astray; but, hereafter, I will be guided by you. I never before heard a fortune-teller who could talk as you do,—you give such good advice."

"I endeavor to use my powers for the good of mankind," said Lucille, solemnly. "I speak only what I know to be true. When I have told you all, you must decide upon your course; and, if you choose the right one, you will, doubtless, be very happy. Be careful that you do not reveal to any one the knowledge you have this day learned from me; when you have heard all, you can tell as much as you please. Farewell, my child; be here promptly at ten o'clock to-morrow, for my time is precious."

Mrs. Thayer withdrew, joined Miss Seaton in the reception room, and they returned home. Lucille then received in rapid succession the visitors who had made appointments the previous day. She had a note-book filled with information obtained by my detectives, and she was thus enabled to satisfy them all immediately; or else, to postpone telling their fortunes until the next day. Then the new arrivals were admitted long enough to tell what they wished to know, after which they each received appointments for the next day. When all were disposed of, Lucille came into the back room to change her dress. I congratulated her upon her success, and was about to withdraw with my stenographer, when the usher came in and said that a gentleman desired an audience. From his description, I felt confident that Captain Sumner was the person who had arrived. I therefore begged Lucille to give him a full sitting, and to read his past for him very thoroughly.

"By the way," I added, "you recollect that while he was away at sea, his sweetheart, Miss Curtis, married a wealthy New York banker, named Agnew. Well, I saw a notice the other day of the death of a banker of that name in New York, and I feel sure that his old flame is now a widow. I want you to refer to this fact in telling his future."

"Oh! well," said Lucille, with some vexation, "I'm rather tired of the business already, and I don't care to spend the whole afternoon in that hot room; so I shall get rid of him as soon as he is satisfied. If you want to tell me anything, make a sound like the gnawing of a rat, and I will come out."

Accordingly, I resumed my place at the door, with my stenographer close beside me, and the Captain was ushered into Lucille's room. She motioned to him to be seated, and then asked, in her most commanding tones:

"What can you learn from Lucille that you have not already learned from the Hindoo of Calcutta?"

The Captain regarded her for an instant in reverent amazement; but, finally, he said:

"I see that you know my past, and that you are truly one of those who can read the fate of others. I am in trouble, and I wish to know when I shall escape from it, if ever. The Hindoo told me much, but I would know more."

Without further conversation, except to ask the day and hour of his birth, Lucille proceeded to pore over a chart and to examine his hand. Finally, she gazed at him steadily a few minutes, and said:

"What I have to say is the truth alone; if it be painful to you, it is because the truth is not always pleasant. Listen calmly, therefore, to the words which the stars declare to be true: Your parents are both dead; your father was a sea-captain, and he brought you up in the same profession. On one of his cruises, a Sepoy presented him with three rings, one of which you now wear; its powers are very great, and it has frequently rendered you important services; take care that you lose it not. It has even saved your life. Yes," she continued, after closely examining the palm of his left hand; "your life has been attempted three separate times lately. You have two sisters living; one of them is happily married and lives in comfort in an eastern State; the other married a sea-captain, but she does not live with her husband. She is with you, and is in poor health. Why! is it possible!" she exclaimed, suddenly. "It was your sister who made the attempt on your life! You may not suspect that your young and charming sister, whom you so deeply love, could have been guilty of such an act; but, unless my powers have failed me so that I cannot read the stars aright, such is the fact. Wait; lest I should have made a mistake, I will try again. It seems too horrible to be believed."

The Captain had buried his face in his hands; but now he looked up and said:

"It is unnecessary to try again; you are right. I see that you are one of the gifted ones of this world, and I wish you to tell me all; I can bear it."

Lucille continued her examination of the Captain's hand as she went on speaking:

"Your sister still has the same kind of poison with her which she used before. She does not intend to use it herself—she has no motive for committing suicide; but she may intend to give it to you again. You must be careful, for that is your greatest danger. Your principal trouble for some time has been caused by that sister. She no longer loves her husband, who has wholly disappeared from your knowledge, and she professes to believe that he is dead. This is not the case, however: he is now in command of an English whaling ship in the South Sea, and he will soon return to England."

At this, the Captain sprang up in a whirl of excitement and joy. In relating the story to me the next day, he said that he felt like taking Lucille in his arms and giving her a genuine sailor hug; but she looked so fierce and wicked that he got the idea that she was a genuine witch; and he was afraid that her beautiful white hands would turn into claws, and that she would soon make a meal of him, if she felt so disposed.

When he sat down again, Lucille again scanned the chart and compared it with his hand. She seemed very much disturbed at the revelations, and, at length, she said:

"Your troubles are so closely interwoven with those of

your sister that I cannot separate them; but I never saw a horoscope so full of frightful scenes — I do not wish to go on with it."

"Please do not stop," said the Captain; "I feel that you have the power to tell me all, and I must know it. I will pay you anything you ask," he added, taking out a roll of money.

"My fees are invariable," said Lucille, drawing herself up haughtily. "You insult me by suggesting that I need to be paid extra to tell the truth."

"I beg your pardon," replied the Captain excitedly; "but I hope you will not refuse to tell me all you know. I can bear it, I assure you."

"Know then that your sister is deeply in love with a very bad man, who lives two or three hundred miles from here. She became acquainted with him in the East and he seduced her, though he was a married man, living with his lawful wife. To quiet your sister's scruples, he had a marriage ceremony performed; but, of course, it had no legal value, since both of the parties were already married. She became *enceinte* by this man, and she caused the premature removal of the evidence of her shame by an abortion. This crime you connived at, though you did not advise it. But the worst is not yet told: this wicked man, finding that you were determined to prevent him from seeing your sister, *resolved to murder his wife*, and to marry your sister legally, supposing that her husband was dead. He accomplished part of his design by poisoning his wife; but he has not yet been able to carry out the whole of his plan. He is now in danger, but he knows it not. He will soon be arrested and tried for murder. If you can succeed in uniting your sister and her lawful husband, they may be able to forget the past and live together happily. All, however, depends upon her. At present she is in deep distress, but the effect of it will be good for her. There is a strong hope that she may be led to see the character of her wicked lover in its true light, and that she may return penitently to the arms of her husband, if he will receive her."

"Oh! he will, I know he will," said the Captain.

"Then, when that happens, your troubles will be at an end. Now I can tell you but little more, as I have a great task to perform, and I must be left alone."

On hearing Lucille say this, I immediately gave the signal, as agreed, and she made an excuse to leave the room for a moment.

"What more do you want?" she asked.

"You have forgotten to tell him about his old sweetheart, Mrs. Agnew."

"Oh! let me skip that," said Lucille impatiently, "I am nearly exhausted, and I cannot stand the atmosphere of that room much longer."

"Just tell the Captain about Mrs. Agnew, and then you will be through work for the day. Try to send him off happy," I pleaded.

"Oh! yes; that is always the way: provided the Captain goes away happy, you don't care what becomes of me. Well, I suppose I must; but I will never undertake such a *role* again."

When Lucille returned to the Captain, he was sitting with his face buried in his hands; but he looked up instantly and asked whether she had anything more to tell him.

She looked at the chart for a few minutes and then said:

"In your youth, you loved a lady of great beauty, and she returned your love; but while you were away at sea, her parents made her believe that you were false to her. They wished her to marry a wealthy banker, and, in a fit of pique, she accepted him. She has always loved you in secret, however, and now that her husband is dead —"

"Is that so?" ejaculated the Captain, springing up in great delight.

"Yes," replied Lucille; "he died a short time ago, and she is now passing her widowhood in New York. She is stouter than she was, but she is still handsome, and she has never ceased to love you. This completes the reading of your horoscope."

The Captain rose to go, but paused to express his feelings. He spoke slowly and with great emotion, since Lucille had completely secured his confidence.

"Madam, I thank you from my heart for the revelations you have made to me. I know that most of the things you have told me are true, and I am satisfied of the truth of the rest also. I should like to pay you in proportion to the value of your words to me." So saying he went out quickly, leaving one hundred dollars on the table.

I found that Lucille's fame was becoming uncomfortably great, since the reception-room was thronged with eager inquirers, who insisted on seeing her, even after the close of her office hours. I, therefore, arranged with Mr. Bangs, my general superintendent, to have a crowd of my own *employees* constantly in attendance, so that outsiders, seeing so many others waiting for an audience, would not remain. By this means, Lucille was able thereafter, to receive as many, or as few, as she chose, and her labors were greatly lightened.

CHAPTER X.

AFTER the interview with Lucille, Mrs. Thayer returned to her boarding-house with Miss Seaton, and invited the latter to spend the day with her. She said that she was low-spirited and wanted company to keep off the "blues." She was very nervous, and she could not take an interest in anything. She said several times that Lucille was the most wonderful person she had ever met, and that she had heard things which convinced her of Lucille's supernatural powers; but she carefully avoided stating anything definite relative to the revelations made to her. Finally she commenced to write a long letter, and Miss Seaton became absorbed in a novel.

After some time the Captain came in, looking very solemn, and Miss Seaton saw that he wished to have a private talk with Mrs. Thayer. Accordingly she rose to leave the room, remarking that she was going down town in the evening and would like to have Mrs. Thayer accompany her. Miss Seaton knew that it was very improbable that Mrs. Thayer would go, on account of the fatigue and excitement of the morning; but she hoped that the latter would give her the letter to put in the post-office. On hearing the approach of the Captain, Mrs. Thayer had hastily concealed her writing materials, thus showing that she was writing to Pattmore. On entering her own room, Miss Seaton took a seat close by a door which connected the two rooms. This door was nailed up and the cracks had been filled with cotton; but she quickly pulled out the filling and obtained an excellent opening to hear all the conversation in the next room.

The Captain first asked his sister when she would be ready to return to Springfield with him. She replied that she would go as soon as she felt able to stand the journey.

"Annie," said he, in an impressive manner, "I fear that you are deceiving me, and that you intend to do me harm. Why do you seek my life? You know that I have done all I could for you, and that I will continue to do so. Why, then, do you wish to poison me? I know that you have poison with you, and that I am the only one for whom it can be intended."

"No, no, you are wrong," replied Mrs. Thayer, in trembling tones; "you are my brother, and why should I wish to injure you?"

"Annie, I know that you have poison about you," said the Captain, firmly, "and I am afraid to remain with you any longer. I have forgiven you once, but now it is my duty to cast you off; *you are plotting to take my life.*"

"Who told you this? What reason have I given you for thinking so?" demanded Mrs. Thayer.

"I have been to see a wonderful fortune-teller, who ——"

The words had no more than passed her lips, when he was interrupted by an exclamation of terror and surprise from Mrs. Thayer, who started to her feet and then fell back upon the sofa, fainting. The Captain was much alarmed at the effect of his remark, and he could not understand why she had fainted at the mere mention of the source of his information. However, he did not spend any time in trying to account for her terror; his first action was to bathe her temples with cold water, in order to restore her to consciousness. When she had partly revived, she lay on the sofa with her eyes closed, as if she had no strength left. Finally she spoke in a weak voice, without looking at her brother:

"Was it a fortune-teller who told you what you have just accused me of?"

"Yes," replied the Captain, "and I know that she speaks the truth."

"My God!" exclaimed Mrs. Thayer, "how could that woman have known that? Well, it is true that I have some poison, though, as God is my judge, it was not meant for you; but, I was resolved that if I could not escape from my present misery, I would take it myself. Never, for an instant, did I intend it for you."

"In either case, Annie, I must have the poison."

Mrs. Thayer rose with great effort, and, going to her trunk, produced a small package labeled " POISON," in conspicuous letters. She handed it to the Captain, and he said:

"I will now destroy this package and thus remove all temptation from you; let us both thank God that you have been prevented from carrying out your design. O, Annie! may this be the last time that I ever shall have reason to doubt you. The fortune-teller whom I mentioned is a wonderful woman. I learned from her many things which I will tell you when you are strong enough to hear them."

"I should like you to tell me very much," said Mrs. Thayer, eagerly; "perhaps she could tell my fortune, if I should visit her."

"Yes, indeed; she could tell you all your past and future; you ought to go there."

"Well, I guess I will try to go to-morrow, if I am strong enough," said Mrs. Thayer.

The Captain kissed her tenderly, and said:

"Annie, never again follow the advice of an evil counsellor; you will never be happy while you continue in a path which you know to be wrong. The fortune-teller had good news for us both, and all will go well if you will only be guided by the wishes of your true friends, who love you and who desire to save you from sorrow."

The Captain then went out and left Mrs. Thayer dozing on the sofa.

In the evening, after supper, Miss Seaton went to Mrs. Thayer's room to see whether the latter wished to take a walk. Mrs. Thayer was not able to go out, but she asked Miss Seaton to put a letter in the post-office for her. Miss Seaton took the letter and brought it straight to Mrs. Warne, who delivered it to me at once. I opened it and read it aloud to my stenographer, who took down its contents as fast as the words fell from my lips.

The letter contained a full account of Mrs. Thayer's second visit to Lucille, and it betrayed great fear of discovery and punishment. She said that she had thought their secret to be perfectly safe, but now she knew that there was at least one person who could disclose their guilt to the world, since that person had the power of finding out everything. She begged him to come to Chicago, to see Lucille, and have his fortune told; he would then learn the wonderful extent of her powers, and would be able to decide what was the best course to pursue. She thought he ought to fly for safety at once, since the fortune-teller predicted that he was in great danger. As for herself, she expected to go East soon, as her brother was anxious to start. If Pattmore did not come to Chicago immediately she might never see him again; she could not bear the idea of separation, but she knew that it must come. It was evident that Mrs. Thayer had wholly forgotten Lucille's injunction to maintain silence upon the subject of her revelations, and I debated an instant whether I should send the letter; but I finally decided to let it go, as he would receive it too late to interfere with my plans, even if he should come to Chicago. I sent a letter to Miller by the same mail, telling him to keep a strict watch on Pattmore, as I feared that he might leave Greenville suddenly. In case of such a movement Miller must telegraph to me instantly.

Miller's reports for several days had been to the effect that Pattmore was working very hard to secure the Congressional nomination, but that he seemed very much troubled about some other matter. He had changed his mind about going West, and had asked Miller to go to Galveston, Texas, with him, in case he failed to get the nomination. Although he still had hosts of friends, he did not confide his plans to any one except Miller. This showed me that there would be but little probability that Pattmore would come to Chicago without Miller's knowledge. That same evening Miller sent me a telegram stating that Pattmore had just received a long letter, evidently from Mrs. Thayer; on reading it he had shown great excitement, and had afterwards become gloomy and dejected to an unusual degree. Miller wished to know whether I had any special instructions about the letter. As this was the letter which Miss Seaton had secured the day before, I replied that he need not trouble himself about it, but that he must keep a close watch upon Pattmore, and endeavor to retain him in Greenville as long as possible.

By the early mail next morning I received a letter from Dr. Stuart, of Greenville; having finished the work upon which he had been engaged, he had begun the analysis of Mrs. Pattmore's bowels; he said that he would let me know the result within a few days.

The whole affair was now gradually drawing to a focus, and I felt confident of a successful termination. I therefore instructed Mrs. Warne to describe me to Mrs. Thayer, and to say that I was watching her movements constantly.

About nine o'clock that morning Mrs. Thayer went out as usual with Miss Seaton, and they proceeded straight to Lucille's rooms. They were the first arrivals, and Mrs. Thayer was admitted to Lucille's presence at once; but Miss Seaton immediately went back to her boarding-house, as I wished to have Mrs. Thayer return home alone. Mrs. Thayer was in a more impressionable state than ever before. The day was dark and lowering, showing every sign of an approaching storm; outside there had been the noisy bustle of active business life, while within the limits of Lucille's mystic chamber all was hushed in a deathly silence. The monotonous swinging of the lamps, the perfume-laden air, the ghastly skeletons, and the imperious bearing and powerful will of Lucille—all struck upon her imagination with resistless force. As she sank into the seat which Lucille pointed out, she felt like a criminal entering the prisoner's dock for trial. She felt that she must relieve herself from her load of guilt or she would forever suffer the torments of remorse.

"Well, my child," said Lucille, in her most solemn tones, "to-day you have come to learn all, and I trust that you have nerved yourself to sustain the revelations which I have to make. I have been through many difficulties and terrible dangers since I last saw you, and a very sad story has been laid before me. Your situation is one of great peril, and upon your own decision this day will rest your hopes of happiness hereafter. Still, you must not be cast down; if you will only resolve to do what is right, your sorrows will gradually pass away, while health and happiness will steadily return to you. Your worst crime was the destruction of your unborn child, for that was a sin against nature herself; but true repentance will save you from the effects of that sin, further than you have already suffered."

This was the first time Lucille had mentioned the fact that she knew of the abortion; yet it seemed perfectly natural to Mrs. Thayer that Lucille should know it; hence, beyond turning very pale at the memory of her suffering, she did not manifest any special emotion on hearing Lucille's words.

The sibyl continued speaking as she gazed, first at Mrs. Thayer's hand, and then at the chart:

"This man, whom you so wrongly love, does not return you the affection of a true husband; he loves you only for selfish, sensual purposes; he will fondle you as a plaything for a few years, and then he will cast you off for a younger and more handsome rival, even as he has already put away his first wife for your sake. If you do not give him up now, some day he will throw you aside or trample you under foot. Think you he will fear to do in the future what he has done in the past? When he wearies of you, have you any doubt that he will murder you *as he has already murdered his wife?*"

Lucille had spoken in a rapid, sibilant whisper, leaning forward so as to bring her eyes directly before Mrs. Thayer's face, and the effect was electrical. Mrs. Thayer struggled for a moment, as if she would rise, and then fell back and burst into tears. This was a fortunate relief, since she would have fainted if she had not obtained some mode of escape for her pent-up feelings. Seeing that there was no further danger of overpowering Mrs. Thayer, as long as she was able to cry, Lucille continued:

"Yes, the heartless villain murdered his wife by poisoning her. I can see it all as it occurred; it is a dreadful scene, yet I know that it must be true—a woman of middle age is lying in bed; she has evidently been very handsome, but now she shows signs of a long illness; your lover, her husband, enters, and he wishes to give her some medicine; but see, she motions him away, though she is unable to speak; she must know that he is going to poison her; yet she cannot help herself, and the nurse does not suspect his design. Now he has given her the poison, and she is writhing in an agony of pain. He professes to be much afflicted, and, oh, heavens! with the treachery of Judas, he attempts to kiss her! Now it is all over; with one last, reproachful look, she has passed to that land where 'the wicked cease from troubling, and the weary are at rest.' She is dead, *and her husband is her murderer.*"

"Oh! for God's sake, spare me, spare me!" exclaimed Mrs. Thayer, between her sobs. "I cannot listen to the description of such a death-bed scene without horror. I know I have been very guilty, but I shall try to make amends in the future. Have pity on me, I beg of you, and do not overwhelm me with such terrible scenes."

"You must hear all," said Lucille, firmly. "There are two more acts in this tragedy to which you must listen; the first is a weird scene in a church-yard by night, and the clear starlight only half reveals the actors; there are three men engaged in digging at this woman's grave; yes, even in death, her body cannot rest in peace. Near by lies the corpse of another woman, whose cold, white face is turned up mutely to the silent stars; now the men reach the coffin and try to drag it from the grave. What is their object? Ah! I see! they wish to substitute one corpse for the other, so that the poison will never be discovered in case of an inquest upon the body of the murdered woman. Suddenly three other men rush upon the grave-diggers before they have been able to pull the coffin from the grave; a chase ensues, and pistol-shots are fired; but finally the resurrectionists escape, though they have been foiled in their purpose. The last scene is the inquest: the coffin is brought in, but the murderer dare not look upon the face of his victim; a sham investigation is held, and he is cleared by the verdict of the jury; but other watchful eyes have been regarding the proceedings; keen detectives have been at work, and they now step in, unknown to the public, and take quiet possession of the corpse; the stomach is removed for analysis, and a chemist of great reputation takes charge of it; poison has been found; positive proof of your lover's guilt have been obtained, and he will suffer the penalty of his crime. You also are in danger, but if you tell the truth, you will be saved."

As Lucille impetuously placed before Mrs. Thayer the occurrences which my investigations had disclosed, it seemed to the latter as if she were the victim of a horrible nightmare. She felt that she was surrounded by unseen foes, who were gradually tightening the toils in which she and Pattmore had become entangled. She was neither brave nor self-sacrificing; she had a sensitive dread of exposure, trial, and punishment, which was aggravated by a knowledge of guilt and an uncertainty as to the extent to which she had become legally liable; also, she had none of the spirit of devoted affection which sometimes prompts a woman to bear the greatest hardships for the sake of the man she loves; hence, she was ready to do anything to save herself, even at the expense of Pattmore's life. As Lucille concluded her terrible recital, Mrs. Thayer shrieked in an agony of remorse and fear:

"Oh, have mercy on me! I am lost! I am lost! Tell

me what I can do to escape punishment; I will obey you wholly—I will do anything you tell me. Oh, save me, save me! I know you can if you will."

It was some time before Lucille could restore her to a quiet state of mind, but at length her sobs ceased and Lucille continued:

"The worst is now past, and if you will return to your brother and confess all, he will forgive you. When you are called upon to tell what you know about this wicked man, you must do so without reserve. You will never see him again except in prison. If you do as your brother wishes, you will regain your light heart and sweet disposition; your real husband will come back to you, and your future will be one of happiness."

Mrs. Thayer sat motionless, with her face buried in her shawl; occasionally a long, choking sob would make her whole frame quiver, but otherwise she gave hardly a sign of life.

"Let me see your face," commanded Lucille.

As Mrs. Thayer slowly raised her tear-stained countenance, Lucille gazed intently into her eyes, and again examined the lines of her hand; then she went on speaking:

"There is another man near you, whose presence you do not suspect; neither have you ever seen him; but he is watching you all the time. You will soon meet him, for he wishes to talk with you. He is only of medium height, but he is very well built and powerful; he has a full face, ruddy complexion, brown hair, and gray eyes; he wears full whiskers all around his face, and his expression is kindly but resolute. He is a very determined man, and when he tries to do anything he never gives up until he has accomplished his object. He has great power, and if you follow his counsel he can save you from harm; but you must trust him fully and tell him the whole truth, for he can instantly detect any falsehood or evasion, and he will be very dangerous to you if you try to deceive him. This is all I have to tell you at present, my child; I wish you well, but I cannot devote more time to you. I hope you will give heed to what I have told you, and that you will decide to follow the right path. There are many now awaiting an audience with me, and I must hasten to admit them, since I cannot tarry long in one city. I have been here now some time, and I must soon journey on; the waste places of the far West call to me—yea, even the deserts of the barren hills. I must plunge into solitude for a time, to commune with Nature."

Then, raising her arms, Lucille placed both hands lightly on Mrs. Thayer's head and said, solemnly:

"May the Spirit of Eternal Truth go with thee, my child, to guide thee forevermore! Farewell."

When Mrs. Thayer looked up, after a few minutes of silence, Lucille had disappeared, having slipped into the room where I and my stenographer were listening. Seeing that the fortune-teller had dismissed her, Mrs. Thayer drew down her heavy veil and left the room. One of my men was stationed at the front door to watch her movements, so that when I joined him, after a few minutes hurried talk with Lucille, he pointed out to me the direction she had taken. I hastened down the street until I caught sight of her; then, seeing that she was on her way

"She was struck almost speechless with fear. She could only ejaculate, Oh! God, help me! that man has come."—Page 231.

back to her boarding-house, I decided not to speak to her just then. The street was quite crowded, and I preferred not to risk having a scene in the presence of so many spectators. Therefore I walked at a safe distance behind her until she was across the bridge; but, on reaching a quiet neighborhood, I overtook her and said:

"Mrs. Thayer, I believe?"

It must be remembered that she had no acquaintances in Chicago except her fellow-boarders; hence my recognition of her would have startled her, even had she never been told to expect me. But, as it was, my appearance gave her a great shock, since she was at that moment revolving in her mind the information given her by Lucille. Therefore, when she was addressed by a stranger, whom she at once recognized as the man about whom Lucille had given her a forewarning, she was struck almost speechless with fear. She could only ejaculate:

"Oh! God help me! that man has come!"

I saw she was nearly ready to faint, so I took her arm and said:

"Mrs. Thayer, I wish you to accompany me to my office."

She was so weak that I supported her a short distance until one of my men, who had remained within call, could bring a hack. I then helped Mrs. Thayer into the carriage and told the driver to proceed at once to my office. Mrs. Thayer said nothing, and showed no objection to my wishes; but she was greatly alarmed, and she could not take her eyes off my face. She had a sort of helpless, questioning look, which I was glad to see, since it was evidence that she was now wholly under my control.

When the carriage stopped, I assisted her to walk up stairs into my private office, where my stenographer had already taken a position to hear without being seen. I gave her a comfortable chair, and handed her a glass of water, for I saw that she was very faint. As soon as her color began to show that she had revived I said:

"Mrs. Thayer, you perceive that I am well acquainted with you. I am sorry that you are in trouble, and I wish to be your friend, if you will allow me to be so; all I ask is that you tell me the whole truth about all your difficulties."

"Are you really my friend?" she asked, in a trembling voice; "can I rely upon what you say, and be sure that you will not take advantage of me? Oh, sir, my heart seems ready to break, and I know not what to think. I am a poor, weak woman, completely in your power."

"You need have no fear of me," I replied, "I know nearly everything relative to your troubles, but I wish you to tell me all the facts; then I shall know precisely what to do to help you. It is possible to raise a criminal charge against you, but it is my desire to prevent that; therefore, you must tell me everything, without any reservation whatever."

"Who are you?" she asked, after a few moments of thought. "You have not told me your name, yet I know you; I have heard of you before, and I know it will be useless for me to try to hide anything from you, but I would like to know your name."

"My name is Pinkerton," I answered, "but I cannot tell you how I know you, nor why I take an interest in your affairs. I wish you to give me a full account of your relations with Pattmore ever since your first acquaintance with him."

I then gave her a glass of wine to strengthen her, and asked her to proceed. As she spoke at first in a very low voice, I professed to be hard of hearing, in order that she should speak loud enough for my stenographer to hear also.

She first referred to her early married life, when she was perfectly happy in Henry's love; then she said that he made several very long voyages, and when he came home he remained only a few days each time. During one of these voyages, she met Pattmore and his wife in Brooklyn, and they became well acquainted. Afterward Pattmore frequently came to Brooklyn alone, and he always spent much of his time in her society. She did not realize the danger of his intercourse at first; but, gradually, he began to make love to her, and, finally, he accomplished her ruin. Thenceforward she was wholly under his control, especially after Henry's desertion of her. He brought her to his own hotel on the plea that she would be company for his wife, and she lived as his mistress, in fact, though not outwardly, until her brother came to take her away. Her brother succeeded in awakening her remorse, and she determined to return to Connecticut with him. Pattmore, however, opposed this action very strongly, and offered to marry her immediately, saying that his wife was sure to die soon from quick consumption, since all her family had died of that disease at about her age. They were therefore secretly married, and she then wrote to her brother that she should not return to Connecticut. When she discovered that she was *enceinte* she was much alarmed, and she again decided to return to her brother after the abortion had been performed, but Pattmore had a strong control over her still. As soon as she was able to go out, after her illness, Pattmore wrote to her to get a certain prescription put up by a druggist. She did so, and then sent the powders to him. In a short time Pattmore came to Chicago and told her that he had arranged to poison his wife. She was very much shocked at first, but he told her that Mrs. Pattmore could only live about a year anyhow, and that she would suffer a great deal during her rapid decline; hence he argued that there could be no harm in hastening her death to save her from many weeks of pain. He said that he had already commenced to poison her, using small doses, so as to break down her system gradually. While he was there Captain Sumner came back from the East, and he was very angry at Mrs. Thayer for permitting Pattmore to visit her. Then Pattmore told her to poison her brother in order that she might inherit his property. This proposition perfectly horrified her, as she really loved her brother; but Pattmore said that they never could live together as long as Captain Sumner was alive, and that he was afraid the Captain would some day get into a passion and kill them both. In this way he worked on her feelings until she agreed to give her brother some of the powder which she had sent to Greenville. Accordingly she made three attempts to poison her brother, but fortunately she was not successful. Pattmore then returned to Greenville, and soon afterward his wife died. He had visited her only once since that time. but they corresponded regularly. He was very guarded in his letters as to what he said about his wife's death, but she knew that he had carried out his plan, because he had told her so distinctly when he last saw her. He said that he had given her small doses every day until she died; but the doctor believed that she had died of dysentery, so that he was all safe.

When she had finished, I said:

"Well, Mrs. Thayer, I suppose you are aware that you are not legally Pattmore's wife?"

"Yes, I am," she said, with a sort of blind persistency; "his first wife is dead, and as I was legally married to him I am now his wife."

"No, Mrs. Thayer," I replied, "I will show you that your pretended marriage was no marriage at all; when it took place Pattmore's wife was alive, and he could not contract a second legal marriage; again, you have no evidence that your husband is dead, and it is therefore probable that you could not marry again legally. Hence, as he *certainly* committed bigamy, and as you *probably* have done the same, there could be no legal marriage between you."

"Yes, Mr. Pinkerton," she acknowledged, sadly, "I know you are right, but still I cling to that belief. If I could be sure that Henry was alive, I should not regard Pattmore as my husband; but, as his wife is dead, and Henry is also dead to me, I shall think that I am Pattmore's wife."

"Well, you can have your doubts set at rest very soon," said I, "for I have received letters from England saying that Henry is on his return from a whaling voyage in the South Sea."

"Is that so?" gasped Mrs. Thayer. "Well, I was told that, but I could hardly believe it. Oh, what shall I do? It was all my fault that Henry left me; he loved me truly, and I once loved him. Oh, if he would only forgive me, and love me, I might hope to be happy again; but I fear he can never pardon the wrongs I have done him."

"Do not despair, Mrs. Thayer," I said; "Henry may be willing to forgive and forget if you show yourself ready to return his affection. However, the first business is to circumvent Pattmore, and you must lend your assistance."

"What are you going to do with me?" she asked, in a timid voice.

"I shall let you go home," I replied; "but I shall keep a strict watch upon your actions, and if you show a spirit of true repentance, I will shield you from the penalties of your crimes. You will be called upon to testify in court against Pattmore, and then your brother will take you to his farm in Connecticut. You can go now, but your brother must come here and become responsible for your appearance when wanted. One thing more, Mrs. Thayer; you are receiving letters from Pattmore every day; now, I wish you to send me all his letters without opening or answering them. If you attempt to deceive me in anything I shall be obliged to put you in prison."

"Oh, no, no!" she said, eagerly; "you can trust me, I assure you, for I know that I am in your power; a fortune-teller told me so."

"Well, well, I don't care anything about fortune-tellers—I never saw one that wasn't a humbug—but you may depend upon it that I cannot be deceived, and I will not be trifled with. You can go home now and tell your brother to come over here to become your security."

So saying, I called a carriage and sent her home in charge of one of my men. On returning to my office, I found Mrs. Warne awaiting me. I complimented her very highly on her success, and told her that she need not continue the business of fortune-telling more than a day or two longer. I told her to be careful not to receive Mrs. Thayer again, however, but to instruct the usher to tell her that Madam Lucille never received any lady a second time after having completed her horoscope.

In about half an hour Captain Sumner came in. I told him that I was now master of the situation, and that I would make a decided move in a day or two.

"Yes," said the Captain, "Annie has told me a great deal, and she says that I must become responsible for her, and guarantee that she shall not leave town. How have you accomplished all this? I cannot understand it."

"Some day perhaps I will tell you all about it," I replied, "but I cannot do so just now. I wish you to bring your sister here to-morrow morning; I will prepare an affidavit for her to sign, and then we shall soon have Pattmore under arrest."

"Well, if you will only have him punished as he deserves," said the Captain, "I shall consider no reward too great for you. He is a snake in the grass, who has ruined my sister, and covered our family with shame. Now I want revenge."

"I shall do all in my power to have him punished," I said; "and I am very well pleased to see the end so near.

By the way, you might write to Mr. Chapman to inform him of our success."

"I will, indeed," said the Captain, enthusiastically; "if it had not been for him, I never should have thought of coming to you, Mr. Pinkerton."

"Well, good-day, Captain; come here with Mrs. Thayer about ten o'clock to-morrow morning."

I immediately placed the facts before my lawyer, and requested him to prepare an affidavit for Mrs. Thayer to make relative to Pattmore's guilt. The next morning it was ready, and Mrs. Thayer swore to the facts as therein set forth. I then told the Captain to remain in Chicago until I should send for him, and that evening I took the train for Greenville.

On my arrival there I called on Dr. Stuart and learned that his analysis had been finished that day. He had found enough poison in Mrs. Pattmore's bowels to make it certain that she had died from that cause, and not from natural disease. I then made an affidavit, charging Pattmore with murder, and I also filed Mrs. Thayer's affidavit in the court. Everything was done quietly, so that Pattmore was arrested before any one except the sheriff and the judge knew that a warrant had been issued. The arrest created immense excitement; a bitter political campaign was in progress, and it was charged, as before, that the arrest was made for political effect. The grand jury was in session, however, and I sent for Captain Sumner and Mrs. Thayer at once. The testimony of Mrs. Thayer, the nurse, and the grave-diggers, made a pretty strong case; but when I clinched the whole matter with the testimony of Dr. Stuart, there was no longer any doubt in the minds of the jury as to Pattmore's guilt. He was immediately indicted for murder in the first degree, and was consigned to prison to await trial.

The trial took place very soon afterward, and the lawyers for the defense made a very strong fight to clear their client. They were successful to the extent of saving him from execution, but he was sentenced to a term of ten years in the penitentiary.

CHAPTER XI.

SOME years after Pattmore was sentenced, I was walking down Broadway, New York, when I happened to meet Captain Sumner. Our greetings were very cordial, and I invited him to visit me at my New York office.

"I shall be very glad, indeed, to come," he said; "I often think of you, and I can never forget how much I am indebted to you. By the way, I should like to bring a friend with me."

"Do so, by all means," I replied; "I shall always be glad to see any of your friends. But how is Mrs. Thayer? Do you intend to bring her to see me?"

"No; she is not in this country now," he answered, with a pleasant smile; "but she was in good health when I last heard from her, and was very happy, indeed. Henry Thayer returned to the United States about a month after we had settled down on my farm, and he immediately came to see me. I need not tell you how delighted he was to find Annie waiting for him. Their old love for each other returned with redoubled power, and now nothing could separate them. When Annie began to speak of her past follies and errors, Henry stopped her instantly: 'No, Annie,' he said, 'let the dead bury the dead — we will live for the future. Our past shall be forgotten except such memories as are pleasant.' They have resided for several years in China, where Henry is a partner in a wealthy firm. They have two lovely children, and life runs very smoothly and pleasantly for them. I know that this great change in her life was largely due to you, Mr. Pinkerton, and I shall never cease to be grateful for your exertions to save her from misery. I owe you still another debt, which I will tell you about to-morrow, when I bring my friend to see you."

"I am very glad to know that Mrs. Thayer is so happy," I said; "give my regards to her when you write. I must hurry on now, Captain, as I have an important engagement; so good-bye. Bring your friend any time to-morrow afternoon."

So saying, I shook his hand and passed on. The next day he came sailing in, with a fine looking lady of middle age leaning contentedly on his arm.

"Mr. Pinkerton," said the Captain, with a very complacent expression, "I'm spliced. Allow me to introduce Mrs. Sumner—lately Mrs. Agnew."

THE END.

www.ingramcontent.com/pod-product-compliance
Lightning Source LLC
Chambersburg PA
CBHW021353230426

43666CB00006B/511